RAILWAYS THROUGH THE VALE OF THE WHITE HORSE

RAILWAYS THROUGH THE VALE OF THE WHITE HORSE

Adrian Vaughan

THE CROWOOD PRESS

First published in 2015 by
The Crowood Press Ltd
Ramsbury, Marlborough
Wiltshire SN8 2HR

www.crowood.com

British Library Cataloguing-in-Publication Data
A catalogue record for this book is available from the British Library.

ISBN 978 1 84797 871 4

Illustrations are from the author's collection
except where otherwise stated.

Frontispiece: The 8 a.m. Cheltenham speeds through
the Vale on its non-stop run from Kemble to Paddington.
Seen here from Challow signal box in 1962. AUTHOR

Typeset by Bookcraft Ltd, Stroud, Gloucestershire
Printed and bound Malaysia By Times Offset (M) Sdn Bhd

Contents

Acknowledgements		6
Introduction		7
Chapter 1	The Route through the Vale	9
Chapter 2	Steventon	14
Chapter 3	Faringdon Road	26
Chapter 4	Wantage Road	34
Chapter 5	Challow	41
Chapter 6	Uffington and Faringdon	49
Chapter 7	Shrivenham	56
Chapter 8	The Stratton Park Halt and the Highworth Branch	61
Chapter 9	Hay Lane and Swindon Junction	67
Chapter 10	Wootton Bassett	75
Chapter 11	The Vale Signal Boxes	79
Notes		155
Index		159

Acknowledgements

I must thank the following kind friends for their assistance:

- Jim Brown for his courtesy in allowing me to quote at length from his book on Challow station, *Jim Brown Remembers his Wartime Boyhood in the Vale of the White Horse.*
- Don Lovelock for his courtesy in providing so many of his photos.
- Austin Attwell and Sandra Cox of Pendon Museum for their kind cooperation in making available to me the Pendon Museum photographic collection. The magnificent Pendon Museum of the Vale of the White Horse at Long Wittenham is a must-visit place for anyone interested in the Vale.
- Michael H.C. Baker.
- Mark Howells, Engineer, Network Rail.
- David Collins, Chris Hall, Alan Pym and Danny Scroggins, all experts on GWR and Western Region signalling.
- Elaine Arthurs, Curator of STEAM, Museum of the GWR at Swindon, for her prompt help on the image of Exeter Street, Swindon.
- R.A. Cooke for his painstaking research published in his *Track Layout Diagrams of the Great Western Railway and BR Western Region*, Sections 20 and 23. I credit information from this source as 'R.A. Cooke, Section 20 or 23' with the page number.

The signal box diagrams were drawn by Signalling Record Society (SRS) experts using official GWR/WR information painstakingly gathered over many years and combined into the SRS's Signal Box Register, volume 1. The diagrams and the register of signal boxes are obtainable from the Society – see the SRS website, www.s-r-s.org.uk

All references beginning Rail, MT and MFQ are to be found at the National Archives, Kew.

A note on measurements
Distances are given in miles and chains, in accordance with the usage of the time. There are eighty chains to a mile, so 1 chain = 22yd.

Introduction

To quote from Miss Eleanor Hayden's 1928 book *Islands of the Vale*, the land of the Vale of the White Horse 'slopes from the setting sun to the dawn'. It was thus perfectly situated to carry Brunel's railway out of the Thames Valley and up to the summit of the route before dropping away into the valley of the Avon.

The 24 miles through the Vale cannot be described as an exciting piece of railway compared with, say, Oxenholme to Shap, or Settle Junction to Ais Gill, but it was, after Reading, where I grew up with what had been the Great Western Railway. That coal-fired, mechanical railway was a handsome thing in itself. Its stations and its signal boxes fitted perfectly into the beautiful landscape, tall with elm trees, dotted with farms, cattle, woodlands, and parallel with the long green line of the Berkshire Downs away to the south – that splendid skyline – where not a single hawthorn or shrub blotched the green velvet but brushy beech plantations clung to slopes and crowned the ridge, complementing the bold line of the hills.

All was handsome, well made, perfectly proportioned in the landscape and the railway that ran through it. A train journey through the Vale was as if through a well-kept garden. The tracks and the

The Vale of the White Horse in 1939.
H.O. VAUGHAN

side banks were perfectly, neatly, cleanly kept by hobnailed sons of Berkshire toil, weather-beaten and true. No weeds, no scruffy shrubs, no brambles, because they burned off the dead grass from winter each spring.

On the south side, just by the fence, were the tall poles of the telegraph system. The poles, with their many crossbars carrying dozens of wires, gave the dignity of height to the route. Sitting on the grass at the lineside one heard the wind singing in the wires, wistful and haunting. From the train the festoons of wire looped briskly up and down as the train sped past them, a perfect accompaniment to the rhythm of the wheels. Through the window, between drifts of the locomotive's exhaust, one saw the wide grasslands. In winter, one might have seen the Old Berks Hunt streaming colourfully across the fields. You would see a lonely homestead here and there, clefts of the steep hillside leading to the ridge and,

clearing the cutting at Uffington, the crowning glory of the Downs – White Horse Hill.

This was where I grew up and learned how to be a railwayman while still at school. It was a timeless place: the railwaymen joined as school leavers and spent fifty years in the job. Nothing much changed, not even the timetable – at least, it changed only a little. Some trains, like the 5.30am Paddington to Penzance had run through the Vale in Brunel's time. But in 1965 the 'white-hot cutting edge of technology' started to cut jobs, cut roots. Sometime soon, we are promised, the picturesque delights of the overhead catenary for electric trains will grace the Vale. The price of progress is high.

I have collected here some history and some photographs to commemorate a gentler time. I hope you will enjoy the result.

Adrian Vaughan
Barney, North Norfolk

Signpost over the Vale in 1965. H.O. VAUGHAN

CHAPTER I

The Route through the Vale

The railway through the Vale of the White Horse is part of the route chosen by Isambard Kingdom Brunel. On 7 March 1833 he was appointed the Surveyor of not one route for a railway from Bristol to London but 'as many [routes] as might appear to offer any advantage peculiar to themselves'. In his diary that evening and until 26 August, he referred to this work as the 'Bristol Railway'. The glorious title of Great Western Railway was used for the first time, as far as can be known, at the top of page 1 of the London Committee of Management's minutes dated 27 August 1833. Brunel was not shown in those minutes as being present but that evening, when he recorded in his diary that he had been appointed Engineer of the line, he also wrote the title for the time.

Railways to connect the two greatest cities in Britain had been proposed in 1824, but these were the work of ordinary men, going by unimaginative ways, winding and hilly. Brunel was unique among the railway engineers in that he was an artist, a dramatist; he loved the exquisite. His biographer, L.T.C. Rolt, wrote that Brunel said 'The railway I shall build will not be the cheapest but it will be the best.' No one living today, including the long-serving archivist of the Brunel Papers at Bristol, Nick Lee, has been able to find the paper on which Brunel wrote that, but, looking at the results of

Brunel's labours, one can see that he intended his railway to be a work of art.

His architecture was either grand or pretty, depending on circumstance, while the route was chosen for high speed and economy of fuel. This had to be achieved without any regard for the formidable engineering difficulties that it would entail. He was particularly aware of the resistance to movement a train encountered even on the level, quite apart from even the slightest rising gradient. He wrote to his directors on this subject on 15 September 1835. Large expense in construction, he pointed out, would be repaid over the years in reduced fuel bills due to having as level a track as was humanly possible. He would engineer a railway that, in 118¼ miles, had 115 miles of track where a gradient of 1 in 660 (8ft/mile) was the steepest – and there was not very much of that.

He also adopted a gauge – the space between the two rails on which the train ran – of 7ft ¼in. His reason for this was that he wanted to use very large wheels: they would revolve more slowly and thus the friction in the axle bearings would be reduced and less fuel would be needed to haul the train. Brunel wrote that, with the wheels outside the carriage, the wheel diameter could be 'unlimited' and therefore to have a floor space of any practical size he would place the rails wide apart. He also stated that placing the carriage body over the wheels 'raises the body unnecessarily high and limits the size of wheel'. In the event he placed the rails 7ft ¼in apart but the wheels were only 4ft in diameter – 6in larger than on other lines.

The reduction of friction resulting from this increase in the usual size was infinitesimal, but the number of passengers that could be seated in these carriages was one-third less than could be seated in the carriages of the London & Birmingham Railway running on the 'narrow gauge' – the 'standard gauge' of Great Britain. At the time Brunel introduced this plan, ball bearings had been invented for thirty-eight years. Ball races on all axles really would have been a great advance, and would have saved the eccentricity of the broad gauge.

The low carrying capacity of the original coaches was quickly rectified. Brunel designed an excellent chassis running on six wheels and placed the carriage bodies – *inconveniently* – over the wheels. The

wheels came through the carriage floors, under the seats, protected by a cowling. Brunel probably ought to have reduced the gauge, too, as the railway was then only 22 miles long, but the 7ft gauge remained.

Brunel's ordinary brick arches over the track were only very slightly higher over the left-hand rail (in the direction of running) than on the other major main lines, which meant that the size of GWR engines was always restricted to standard gauge height. Broad gauge express engines were, for a time, the fastest in the world but this was due to the skill of their designer, Daniel Gooch: his broad gauge boilers and cylinders could just as easily have been carried on standard gauge axles.

From Wootton Bassett, 83 miles from Paddington, the Great Western line climbs at 8ft/mile for most of the way to the summit of the whole route – Swindon – 77¼ miles from Paddington. Swindon station is approximately 320ft above sea level,[1] 290ft above

Childrey Reading Room, 1963.

Bristol Temple Meads and 270ft above Paddington. About 150yd west of the platforms the railway crossed above the North Wiltshire Canal on a 34ft span bridge that was formed with cast-iron girders. These double and single flange girders, five in all, were cast by Perry & Bassett at their Katesgrove Foundry in Reading on 24 August 1840; they were 'proved' by being loaded at their centres with 21 tons of pig iron. When the canal was abandoned, the tunnel under the railway became a subway to the locomotive works. The ancient beams are still supporting the tracks.

From Swindon to Paddington the line is downhill or level for almost the entire distance – there is a rise and fall of 4ft/mile between West Drayton and Southall to lift the line over two crossings of the Grand Union Canal. This is 'Brunel's Billiard Table', the Great Western's 'Galloping Ground'. Leaving Swindon, the line was designed to fall eastwards at 6ft/mile for 4¾ miles, followed by 2 miles falling

5ft/mile, then level for 1½ miles to the 69 mile post, where Knighton level crossing gates used to be and where it crosses the 300ft contour. From here it falls 8ft/mile, level and 7ft/mile, through to Steventon, at the 56½ mile post. At 53 miles 23 chains from Paddington – just west of Didcot station – the line crosses the 200ft contour.

There are no exceptionally heavy earthworks in the Vale. Perhaps the tallest embankment is that between Marston and the twin arch 'Acorn Bridge' at the 72 mile 60 chain point. Each span is of 38ft 2in, carrying the railway over the Swindon–Oxford road and the Wiltshire & Berkshire Canal. The railway crossed the canal again at about the 68 mile 50 chain point; this was another cast-iron beam bridge, of 20ft 9in span, making a short tunnel through the embankment. The deepest cutting is at Baulking, extending from 66 miles 60 chains to 65 miles 60 chains; the deepest section of this is 35ft for about 200yd. The bridge carrying the Uffington–Baulking

Childrey pond, 1963.

11

road crosses the cutting at its deepest part with a brick arch of 29ft 6in span. At the 63¾ mile post the line passes the site of Challow station. The GWR staff cottages are on the north side, and 2 miles to the south is the village of Childrey: the station is just outside the parish boundary and so missed being called 'Childrey'.

The line continues eastwards on moderate embankments and shallow cuttings, crossing the canal for the last time at 59 miles 27 chains, a lonely spot in the wide open, fen-like fields. The bridge was named 'Ardington' after the village 2 miles to the south. Lying alongside the low embankment on the north side of the line, east and west of the canal bridge, are the mysterious 'Cuttings', so named by local railwaymen. Their position suggests that they were dug to provide spoil to build the embankment, although the railway did not take possession of the land in which the cuttings are located until May 1841. Maybe the company paid the then landowner for permission to dig there in 1839–40 and then had to buy the water-filled pits.

Ardington was another bridge of cast-iron beams, cast by Perry & Bassett. There were two spans, one of 12ft 2in over the tow path and the other 25ft 5in over the canal. Brunel did not remove these cast-iron beams after he expressed his distrust of such things after the Dee bridge disaster of May 1847. The Ardington bridge was taken up and the canal beneath filled in on 17 November 1955. The embankment runs into ordinary ground level a mile before Steventon station, and enters a cutting at 56½ miles where we must turn back into the Vale.

The Great Western Railway route, approved by I.K. Brunel and George Stephenson, was authorized by an Act of Parliament and received the Royal Assent on 31 August 1835.

Having argued – at great expense – in Parliament for this splendid line and having gained the Act, Brunel had second thoughts. He now realized that the land was falling downhill north of where the line was to cross the North Wiltshire Canal at Swindon. This was amply shown by the existence, a mile north of the line, of the first of the twelve locks that dropped the waterway into the Thames

Valley. He realized that he could have a summit level nearly 15ft lower by bringing the railway across the canal north of this lock. This would allow him to have one gradient – rising 6ft/mile – all the way from Steventon to Swindon and the same – but falling – to a point a mile or so beyond the eventual site of Wootton Bassett station.[2]

He was also dissatisfied with his authorized route in that it had a variety of curves from about the 65 mile post which, on the map at least, do look untidy – certainly Brunel had come to dislike them. The deviation he wanted would make a line running in one, very wide, arc, fully in keeping with the shape of the route east of Steventon to London.

The Parliamentary line passes Steventon on an exactly east–west line but, just after it crosses the Wiltshire & Berkshire Canal, it starts a curve slightly south of west, climbing the natural swell of the ground as the line moves closer to the Berkshire Downs. Brunel proposed a deviation that continued due west from the canal bridge, keeping the line in the lower lands and passing close to Denchworth and Goosey where the deviation would be ¾ mile north of the authorized line. The higher ground through which the Baulking cutting was authorized to be made was less high ¾ mile further north. Shallow cuttings would suffice from there and across the face of Barrowbush Hill, south of Fernham. The deviation would cross the Longcot branch of the canal, which Brunel felt sure was of little use, and pass very close to Shrivenham village.

The deviation would slightly increase the distance between Bristol and London, but it would have had a continuous gradient of 6ft/mile and only one long, and imperceptible, curve. Brunel estimated the cost of the deviation at 'an additional £16,000 to £18,000 over the old line'. He tried hard to have his change of mind accepted, but GWR's Lord Barrington objected as the deviation would pass very close to his mansion at Beckett Park, on the eastern edge of Shrivenham. Brunel bombarded him with very polite letters, but Barrington did not want the railway close to his house – even though the tracks would be in a shallow cutting. Barrington

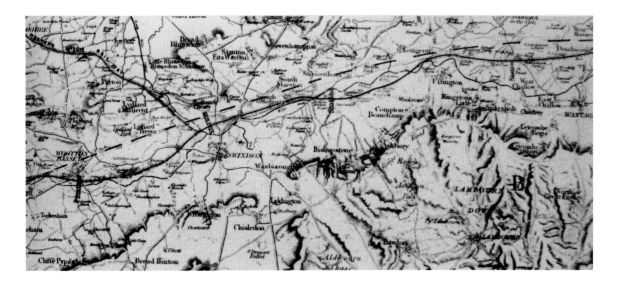

Brunel's proposed deviation.

was a director of the GWR's London Committee of Management, and the London Committee was not – like the Bristol Committee – under Brunel's spell. The railway through the Vale was laid out on the route authorized by the 1835 Act.

The route was divided into five construction contracts, 1S to 5S ('S' for 'Swindon'), from 'Dudcot'(sic) to Lydiard Tregoze, just east of Wootton Bassett. In a massive ledger[3] the names of those contractors who tendered for the works are given, the price they each quoted and the name of the contractor winning the contract. There are no dates, though it is known that the book was started in 1835. Undated, the book also lacks, in some instances, a full heading to a page – as if the clerk writing it was called away to something else and forgot to complete the entry. Some descriptions of the extent of a contract are incomplete.

As far as the Vale route is concerned, the first contracts must have been let towards the end of 1838 because it was in June 1838 that Brunel wrote to his directors recommending that they adopt the deviating route. The idea was rejected and only then could contracts be advertised and awarded:

- No. 1S was from 'Dudcot [sic] Bridge No. 16 to the west bank of the Wilts & Berks canal'. This went to Mr E. Jackson for £35,000 and included the canal bridge.
- No. 2S, from the west bank of the canal (the page heading is incomplete, so the exact end is unknown) went to Richard Cogswell. The price offered is not recorded but the next, higher, price, from William Oldham, was £48,295.
- No. 3S was from a field near Uffington to a field near Woolstone, possibly to where the Woolstone–Longcot road was to cross the railway. This went to Mr S. Simpson for £18,082. His was the only tender
- No. 4S was awarded to Thomas Bedborough for £58,700. (Bedborough was the contractor who built the Maidenhead bridge.) No. 4S was from a field east of Shrivenham to the east bank of the North Wiltshire Canal – the summit of the line.
- No. 5S took in the bridge to be made over the North Wiltshire Canal and onwards to a field near Lydiard Tregoze, east of Wootton Bassett. Only one man tendered for the work: William Oldham, quoting £20,539.

CHAPTER 2

Steventon

The GWR directors were undecided about what stations they would need in the Vale. It was a lonely place and the line did not pass close to either of the Vale towns (Wantage and Faringdon). In 1840 they decided on three: Steventon, 56¼ miles from Paddington; Faringdon Road, 63¼ miles; and Shrivenham, 71 miles. These are the pre-1855 mileages; when the existing Paddington station was opened in 1854, ¼ mile had to be added to mileages.

The station office building at Steventon was on the north-side platform – the Up side. The contract drawing for the station office shows an entirely wooden building with a low-pitched roof with hipped ends. Along the length of the office, covering the width of the platform, was a steeply pitched roof on wooden columns. A canopy was cantilevered out over the entrance to the building on the yard side. The simple wooden shed design implies a temporary job and the station did have a temporary roof. A minute of the GWR General Committee of 3 May 1842 states:

> Considered a tender by Mr Abbott, the contractor, for removing the present, temporary roofing at the Steventon station and Faringdon Road stations and substituting slate at the following prices: Steventon £48; Faringdon Road £78.[1]

The station building was only intended as a temporary structure but the rest of the station's building were built solidly in brick and stone.

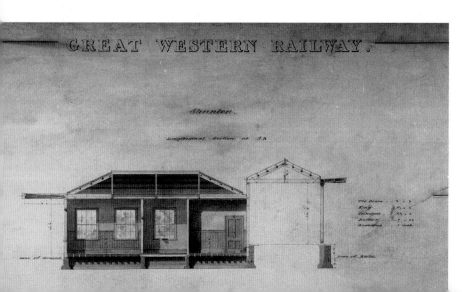

Steventon station contract drawing, 1839.

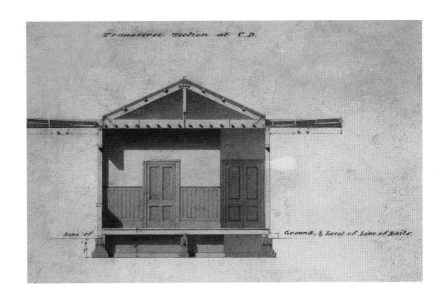

Steventon station contract drawing, cross-section.

Parallel to the south side of the railway, a few yards beyond the west end of the Down platform, there was a terrace of '9 cottages of railway brick under slate roofs'. Of these, seven formed a terrace of what must have been dark and cramped single-storey dwellings, in a Tudor style on the outside. At each end of the single-storey terrace were two-storey, 'Tudor' gabled houses: at the east end the gables faced east and north, and at the west end west and north. A 'Superintendent's House' and a 'Public House' are shown in elevation on the contract drawings of 1840. The 'Public House' was not built.

Steventon

RIGHT: Superintendent's house contract drawing, 1839.

BELOW: Steventon workmen's cottages. Contract drawing.

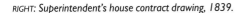

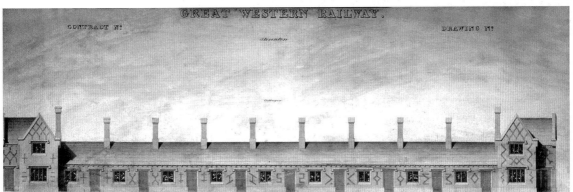

Steventon hotel/superintendent's house, south gable, 1971.

Steventon hotel/superintendent's house, east side, 1971.

Steventon hotel/superintendent's house, west side, 1971.

Brunel employed J.H. Gandell as his architect for Steventon and also as Resident Engineer to supervise the six contractors of the Vale route. Gandell had been a Resident Engineer under Robert Stephenson on the London & Birmingham Railway, and when the L&BR was complete and opened, in June 1838, Gandell was taken on by Brunel – with a glowing reference from Robert Stephenson. Gandell had an architectural practice with offices at Wolverton on the London & Birmingham Railway. He was ultimately responsible for developing the external and internal design of the housing at Steventon. J. & C. Rigby built Steventon station office building and all the original stations through to Swindon inclusive.

Gandell, like Brunel, had assistants in his office who worked out the detailed construction plan and produced the finished drawings: Brunel made sketches and Gandell or his assistants actually made the designs. This was normal practice – the terminal office buildings at Bristol Temple Meads were sketched by Brunel, and the design and working drawings for the builders were developed in the office of an architect called William Westmacott. This can be seen in a letter from Brunel to Westmacott at the National Archives.[2]

Gandell and his employees were working for Brunel's project and Brunel was charged according to Gandell's costs. Brunel kept a very close watch on costs. He decided Gandell was charging too much for his services and on 13 April 1839 he wrote to Gandell:

> In looking over the quarter's expenses I find that yours is the heaviest by far in proportion to the work in hand of any upon the line – your establishment of draftsmen is out of all reason. You have as the Head one who was formerly with me at Duke Street – Freeman – but who was actually too expensive – you must get rid of him and reduce your establishment very considerably.[3]

Gandell wrote back saying Brunel was being 'tyrannical' and said that he, Gandell, would not sack such a good man but would pay Freeman from his own pocket. Brunel was not satisfied with that fair way out of the problem. He resented Freeman and wanted to hurt him. Brunel replied, denying tyranny, and wrote:

> as to your doing such a foolish thing as paying Freeman yourself you will oblige me very much by plainly telling him the state of the case and giving him fair and reasonable notice.

That Brunel assumed he had the authority to order Gandell how to spend his own money is a mystery of vendetta. Whether Gandell did as Brunel ordered is not known, but he swallowed the insult and continued as both an architectural contractor and as a Resident Engineer for the Steventon–Wootton Bassett section. Brunel's letters to him are often verbose to the detriment of clarity and carry an oddly superior tone. On 20 April 1839, he wrote to Gandell:

> The gradients as sent to you by Mr Clarke are the result of rather a laborious and careful balancing of all the quantities and other considerations which I am in the habit of going into myself before they are finally fixed upon for the contracts and you cannot, my dear Sir, suppose that I would neglect such reviews merely because the sections and calculations were ready on the old line, besides, they are also all ready as the gradients are now fixed by me – I mentioned this in my letter of yesterday but clearly understand that this does not in any way influence my decisions.
>
> You evidently do not at all understand me but I have no doubt when we know each other better we shall get on very well. I shall endeavour and go into all these matters – as regards the bridges in these contracts – you will of course maintain exactly the same character as in the bridge of No. 1 and 2S. The bridges under the railway may be exactly like them the bridges over must be similar to Drawing No. 7 Pangbourne contract adopted of course to the particular cases – slopes etc but the form of the main arch to be constant and exactly like No. 7 being 15ft 3in over the outside rail or at 10ft 2in from the centre, the course of the extrados or of the string course to be governed by the inclination of the ascent (if any) of the road.

> - Turnpike road 1 in 30
> - Parish road 1 in 20
> - Occupation road 1 in 20

> Widths between parapets at the plinth
> - Turnpike, 18ft
> - Parish, 15ft 2in
> - Occupation 14ft

I have made some alterations in pencil on the Drawing No. 7 – this arrangement of three arches ought to have been followed in 1S and 2S and I don't remember why it was not – I must talk with you about altering them.

I enclose you a statement of the diversions of your next three contracts with the bridges required in the contracts let me know immediately how many and which you can prepare. In giving the angles of the skews we want the angle from a line square to the rails so that 0 degree would be a square bridge and the example above would be a 20 degree left and this a 20 degree right.

The three roads at Stratton St Margaret are to be deviated as shewn in a tracing Mr Clarke will send you and the bridge is preparing here.

You must prepare the specifications and have them ready by the end of the week that we may have time to examine.

You will see to this yourself that you may thoroughly understand the whole

No. 2 S

By a slight alteration in the line of rails and the cross section of the Baulking cutting the contract will extend beyond the Uffington Road as far as about 60,000 (cubic) yards will go – and from that point begin No. 3S

Between 3 and 4S is a space not included in either – this we will arrange for with one of the contractors or let to local people.

The canal bridge at the Swindon summit and the bridges beyond this need not be got out at present.

You will take care and shape all your brickwork to correct dimensions of 9 inch bricks.[4]

Gandell eventually found Brunel's lectures too much and he resigned early in February 1840. On the 11th, Brunel wrote to him in the most friendly way:

I have informed the directors of your resignation. I have great pleasure in assuring you that I have been perfectly satisfied with your conduct as my Assistant and that I regret that circumstances should have rendered it necessary that you should leave the works – which you do with perfect credit to yourself.

That part of your district comprising Contracts Nos. 1 & 2S which is now nearly completed and upon which the laying of the permanent rails and preparations of the stations is the principal work remaining to be done will be placed under the charge of Mr Hammond. As to the part beyond the Faringdon Road and in the Bristol Division it is not settled what will be done and I wish to have some further conversation with you. I shall be at Steventon on Thursday next at about 2 o'clock when I should wish to meet you.[5]

Gandell continued his work for Brunel as the contractor for designing and erecting the Steventon domestic buildings he had largely designed: on 26 November 1840 Brunel wrote to Gandell, referring to the Steventon houses as 'your houses'. Brunel wrote to Gandell twice on 23 April 1840:

[The first letter said:] I am sorry to have to complain very seriously of the delay at Steventon. We shall open that place on 1 June and there will evidently be neither cottages for our men or stables or any other of those accommodations which you have undertaken to supply. I can assure you this will seriously injure your position with the company. If you can make great exertions and retrieve lost time I would advise you to do so.

[The second letter said:] The business at Steventon will require a larger [illegible – A.V.] than I had provided and certainly the Superintendent, Mr Bell, with a wife and a dozen children cannot live in the house I had proposed.[6]

Gandell was told to enlarge the original plan for the superintendent's house.

On 27 April 1840, a letter from Brunel to Gandell gives us a fine insight into the hours that Brunel worked:

Mr Saunders [the company Secretary] and myself will be at Steventon a little before 6am on Wednesday morn, at Wantage (Bear Hotel) for breakfast at 7 and at the Leather Bottle inn at 8. [This was half a mile north of the then-under-construction Faringdon Road station.] I wish particularly to meet you with your plans for the cottage etc.

To carry out that itinerary on horseback would have required some hard galloping and possibly they did that across the fields as a shorter route than following the roads.

Gandell produced the new plans for the superintendent's house on 12 May. Brunel was aghast when he received them and wrote at once:

> The plans you have sent me for the Superintendent's house have arrived late and have been printed in reverse. You must use the plans in reverse.[7]

In spite of the negligible progress noted by Brunel in April, the station cottages and stabling were ready on time for the advertised opening. The railway was extended from Reading to Steventon on Monday 1 June 1840. The day before that the Great Western directors had a private view. The *Berkshire Chronicle* of 6 June described the private view and public opening thus:

> This great national work having been completed on Saturday last to Steventon the station was the scene of much animation and bustle. Knowing it was the intention of the directors to visit the station on

Sunday a considerable concourse of persons flocked to witness the, to them, novel mode of locomotive conveyance.

At half past 12 o'clock the directors and a large party of ladies, amongst whom we recognized Lady Barrington, arrived at the station in a train of 1st class carriages which were preceded by a splendid new engine, the Charon. Among the directors we noticed Mr Charles Russell, late MP for Reading, the Chairman of the Board of directors, the Viscount Barrington MP, Mr Brunel, the Engineer and Mr Saunders, the company Secretary. The directors, having inspected the works, with which they appeared highly satisfied, retired with their friends to the Station House where they partook of a cold collation after which they returned by the same train to their respective places of destination. The journey from London to Steventon was performed in the almost incredible time of 70 minutes.

Monday being the day announced for the opening to public traffic, vast numbers of stage coaches, omnibuses and every other description of vehicle were to be seen from an early hour of the morning until night, wending their way in all directions to and from the scene of the attraction, where, about the middle of the day, thousands of people had congregated to gratify their curiosity. The day was fine and never before was witnessed in the quiet village of Steventon so animated a picture – the whole, from the number of booths and the vast mass of

Steventon station from the Down side. The hotel-cum-superintendent's house in centre distance, 1964.
PENDON MUSEUM

Steventon station, from the Up side, looking west, 1964. PENDON MUSEUM

Steventon station 1840 office on Up platform, 1964. PENDON MUSEUM

The rear of the 1840 station office, 1964. PENDON MUSEUM

persons collected together having the appearance of an extensive fair. As a matter of course there was a goodly sprinkling of that mysterious class of persons, gypsies, following their customary callings.

At about half past 10 in the forenoon the first train arrived, with the elegant and unique engine the Leopard, containing a large number of passengers from the metropolis and elsewhere, having performed the journey from the former place in a little more than two hours.

Steventon engine house must have been equipped with a locomotive turntable, water and coke supply. Charon and Leopard were 'Firefly' class engines designed by Daniel Gooch, the GWR locomotive superintendent. The Charon was built by Fenton, Murray & Jackson in Leeds and delivered to the railway in May 1840. The Leopard was built by Sharp Roberts & Co. of Manchester, and also arrived on the railway in May 1840. The 'Fireflies' were a very effective design and worked for the company for many years. They were of the 2-2-2 variety – a pair of 4ft carrying wheels fore and aft and a pair of 7ft driving wheels in the middle, giving a wheelbase of 13ft 2in. The maximum boiler pressure was only 50lbs.psi working on two 15in diameter pistons with a stroke of 18in.[8]

To have travelled 56¼ miles in 70 minutes is an average of 48mph. The tonnage hauled is unknown except that in 1840 a 'First Class' carriage was a long wheelbase six-wheeler weighing 7½ tons; it had four compartments in a 24ft body and could accommodate thirty-two people. The size of the party is not known, but if there were thirty-two guests, there may have been two carriages to avoid cramming the compartments. Maybe the tonnage hauled was 20 tons. To have covered the distance in the time recorded required speeds approaching – or even reaching – 60mph.

The speed is a great tribute to Daniel Gooch's design of the locomotive and in that regard it should also be noted that the journey was accomplished on one tender-full of water and coke, which really does show what a good design the 'Fireflies' were. There is no record of the water capacity of these early

tenders, but experienced steam footplatemen alive today imagine they were 'cutting it fine'.

On 15 October a railway enthusiast and train timer, Mr J. Lock, took a train from Paddington to Steventon. Mr Lock wrote to the directors:

I took an expedition down the Great Western yesterday to Steventon. We started by my watch at 12 hours 10 minutes and did not arrive until 2 hours 55 minutes and it was by no means a heavy train. (56¼ miles in 175 minutes = 20.45mph.) We left Steventon at 3 hours 21 minutes and did not arrive at Paddington until 6 hours 24 minutes from having a heavy train (18.75mph). The times are taken from my watch not your clocks.

The comfort of your [1st class?] carriages and steadiness of action continues to exceed that of any other railway but you lose a great deal of time at stations and you should take an extra engine to meet such an eventuality such as mine yesterday.

The day before I left the Vauxhall (Nine Elms) station at 10.5am and arrived at Southampton, 77 miles, at 1 hours 5 minutes (25.6mph) keeping time with the utmost precision throughout. I returned at 3 precisely and got to Vauxhall as it was striking 6. I have never seen the same precision in any railway that I have travelled on and I have been upon every one in England. The directors deserve great credit for this exactness.

Gandell was paid for his work at Steventon in July 1840. Brunel wrote to him on the 8th:

I have sent Mr Saunders my certificate of the completion of the cottages and stabling. You must undertake, however, that fires shall be burnt in them daily until they are dry as it would not be safe for the men to come into them in their present state.

On 30 July 1840, with the line open from Bristol to Bath and from Steventon to Faringdon Road but with forty-three intervening miles yet to be completed, the directors met to consider how the railway, once fully opened, would be organized and managed.

These arrangements need not concern us except for the entry on page 131 of Rail 250/2, where they resolved that 'the monthly meetings of the Board to be held on the first Tuesday of each month and alternately at London, Bristol and Reading'. This resolution proved very inconvenient to keep and on pages 202–3 of the minutes for 5 October 1841 it was resolved that 'all Meetings of the Board or of the two Committees be held at Steventon if the requisite offices can be provided there without material expense to the company'.

Gandell had been instructed to enlarge the superintendent's house by Brunel on 23 April 1840. Reading the minute of 26 January 1842, it seems unlikely that it was enlarged, because that minute reads:

Read a letter from Mr Dawkes to Mr Bailey of Berners Street with plans for a proposed alteration of the Steventon buildings by substituting the present hotel for the Superintendent's House in order to obtain two Committee rooms as well as Superintendent's dwelling – the Secretary instructed to write to Mr Bailey on the subject.[9]

The order to make the hotel the superintendent's house is confusing because according to a minute of 6 April 1841 the Steventon hotel was leased to a third party. This minute reads:

Read letter from William Dunsford Esq, upon the subject of building an Hotel at Shrivenham ... the company will be happy to entertain any proposal from him for a Building Lease to be granted upon terms similar to that at Steventon.[10]

This minute shows that the Steventon railway station hotel was built by a private individual on land leased from the company and yet it was used as the dwelling for the company's employees and as a directors' meeting place.

Did Mr Dunsford build his hotel on GWR land at Shrivenham? Just outside the entrance to the station yard there still stands a public house which was 'The Victoria' in 1962. It is quite large enough to have

been a hotel. The 1875 GWR survey[11] of Shrivenham station shows a 'Tavern' in that position, outside the company boundary but with a GWR-owned path leading from the tavern to the station.

The directors' Traffic Committee first used the rooms in the hotel-cum-superintendent's house on 4 August 1842[12] and every two weeks thereafter until 3 November 1842.[13] But the fact that the building had been used as a boardroom was never forgotten and this was pointed out to me by the Steventon signalman in 1960.

Steventon never rose above the rank of 'wayside station' – except in one particular. From 30 July 1841 Steventon became a stopping place for the three mail trains each way between Paddington and Bristol, inaugurated in that year. Mail to and from Oxford was very conveniently conveyed by the turnpike road. For the next 123 years the Up and Down mail trains, including the Travelling Post Office express mails, stopped at Steventon. In 1863 the 12.35am Bristol 'Special Mail' with letter-sorting coaches stopped at Steventon every morning at 2.40am. In 1929 the 6.48pm Penzance stopped there from 2.30 to 2.35am. In 1964 my friend, relief Porter Harry Strong, who by then must have been sixty years old, frequently cycled from his cottage in Standford-in-the-Vale to Steventon to open the station at 2.15am to permit the Post Office men to load and unload mail. He locked up a few minutes later and cycled home.

The station staff employed at Steventon in 1863 consisted of: station master earning £80 a year, three policemen earning 16/-, 15/- and 19/- a week respectively, a gateman on 14/- a week and a porter on 17/-. The annual wage bill for the station was £488 4s 0d.[14]

To the west of the station there were three level crossings: Stocks Lane at 56 miles 60 chains; Causeway at 56 miles 72 chains; and Berrycroft at 57 miles 6 chains. There was also a footpath crossing the tracks between Stocks Lane and Causeway. Four crossings, but only four men to open and shut the gates. There was a small two-storey cottage close to the Up main line at Stocks Lane crossing. It is shown on the GWR two-chain survey of 1875.

The gateman tenant and his wife could attend to the gates twenty-four hours a day, seven days a week. That left two more crossings and only three policemen. Two men were required at the station, one for day and one for night duty, to operate the disc and crossbar signals, leaving one man to work the Causeway crossing. This man could only do one twelve-hour shift, leaving the crossing unattended for twelve hours each day or night. I must assume that the GWR wages list is correct and so the crossing 286yd west of Causeway was not guarded at all: this was definitely the case at the Circourt crossing, 5 miles to the west.

Between Steventon and Longcot level crossing – sixty-ninth mile post – the station policemen, gatemen and policemen on mobile 'beats' were supervised by Inspector Wells from 1840 to 1845. He was an unpopular man, not entirely because of his strict supervision but because the men knew he was 'on the take'. On 9 February 1842, Policeman Barefoot of Steventon was called before the directors at Paddington charged with writing an anonymous letter accusing Inspector Wells of improper conduct and keeping back money from

supernumerary policemen which, upon investigation, was disproved. He was therefore dismissed.[15] On the same day, Tuck, another Steventon policeman, was charged with having written, using the name of Boseley, a fraudulent character reference for a man called Higgs who wanted employment as a policeman. The fraud was discovered and Tuck was dismissed.

The London Division superintendent, Mr Kelly, was at Steventon in October 1845 when Constable Scarborough allowed a wagon to be placed on the line but did not turn his crossbar on to protect it. Scarborough appeared before the directors on the 30 and admitted the misdeed. The directors took into account his previous good record and did not dismiss him but fined him 10/- – to be deducted from his wages over four weeks – and cautioned him for the future.

Also appearing before the directors that day was Inspector Wells, along with the man who had the contract to run the goods yard, that man's employees and the two Steventon constables. Wells was charged with stealing timber from wagons and the constables for failing to report him. It was revealed

Steventon Stocks Lane crossing keeper's cottage, 1965.

that both constables lodged at the Inspector's house, which was against the company's rules. The directors were particularly shocked by the whole case and deferred making any decision until their next meeting a month later; the outcome was that Wells and the two constables were sacked.[16] Given the ordinary short-staffing of the stations, one wonders where the relief signalmen came from while the accused staff were at Paddington – and how quickly the company could replace the men they dismissed.

Working on the railway was an entirely new experience. What was required of a railwayman had to be learned. The nearest thing to it was working on the stage coaches – and the sort of 'free-for-all' that existed between the coach drivers, guards and passengers would not work on the railway.

The Great Western was 'the gentleman's railway' according to the locomotive superintendent, Daniel Gooch, who became Chairman of the company in 1865. All employees, whether they were dealing with the public, attending to the safety of the line or working in an office, were expected to behave as if they were working in 'gentleman's service'. They were bound by the Rule Book to 'see that the safety of the public is their chief care under all circumstances' and to 'be prompt, civil and obliging, afford every proper facility for the company's business, give correct information and, when asked, give their names or numbers without hesitation.' In the 1840s and 50s these were entirely new concepts to a great many of the men coming onto the railway, who still had robust, eighteenth-century attitudes.

Steventon station had 13–16 people on its wage bill through the period 1903–38. The accompanying table is a simplified extract from GWR statistics. There is no need to give data for every year – the trend is one of decline.

The table shows increases in pay but also that increases were made simply to keep in step with inflation. The wage bill's more than doubling between 1913 and 1923 is the effect of wage rises to compensate for the equivalent decrease in the purchasing power of money due to the First World War. The economic depression of the late 1920s into the 1930s is also shown. The apparent increase in 'goods' income is actually a decrease because the figures are not equal to post-war inflation. After several years of dwindling income the GWR and all railway companies reduced wages by 2½ per cent from 26 March 1931 – provided that no wages grade man was paid less than £2 a week. The 2½ per cent reduction was abolished on 15 August 1937.

Steventon station was closed for all purposes on 5 December 1964.

Steventon passenger/parcels statistics[17]

Year	No. of staff	Annual wage cost £	Total passenger income £	Tickets sold	Season tickets	Goods income £
1903	14	968	6060	10747	nil	4237
1913	16	1113	10553	12512	nil	7822
1923	16	2667	11345	12600	17	8307
1929	14	2289	7675	7382	9	5581
1930	14	2309	5777	6078	12	3841
1933	13	2090	4042	4357	4	3118
1938	14	2540	4214	3885	5	2699

RIGHT: *Looking east on the Up platform in 1964, through the arch of the broad gauge 1840 bridge. A gantry for the new colour-light signals can be seen on the Downside.*
PENDON MUSEUM

BELOW: *A Churchward '28' class goods engine freewheels through the station on the Up main at the head of an 'H'-headcode unbraked train bound for the Up goods loop, 1964.*
PENDON MUSEUM

Looking west on the Up platform, lens somewhat into the sun in 1964. The 1840 terrace of railwaymen's cottages on the Down side with Stocks Lane signal box beyond.
PENDON MUSEUM

CHAPTER 3

Faringdon Road

The railway was extended to the Faringdon Road station, 63 miles 50 chains from Paddington, on 20 July 1840. This was achieved without a visit from the directors. The station main building was on the north side of the line, the platforms abutting the brick arch bridge that carried the Gloucester–Reading turnpike road above the railway. On the south side of the road bridge, 100yd down the slope, was the toll gate and toll house for the Wantage–Faringdon turnpike toll collector. The turnpike trust expired in 1873. The railway station office was very similar in appearance to Steventon except that Faringdon Road was a longer building to accommodate a refreshment room. This is shown by the prices asked by the contractor, Abbott, to replace the temporary roofing here and at Steventon. The record of insurance states that the Faringdon Road goods shed was 'a timber building clad in timber'. The station was insured for £1,000.[1]

Looking west over what became the Up main and Up relief lines in 1933. The 1905 vintage 'pagoda' corrugated iron waiting shelter was painted and removed to the new Up platform, east of the bridge. Some detail of the 1840 station can be seen. The white-painted drinking water tank is next to the fence.

On the level land from the western verge of the turnpike road a space for a market was established about 80yd northwards, alongside the road and 50yd along the base, near and parallel to the station building. Here sales of wheat, cattle and sheep took place for decades to come, the dealers arriving by train and their purchases being sent away by train. On 8 February 1845 a corn market was held there and the 8am Paddington was stopped specially for the benefit of dealers. The GWR two-chain survey of 1875 shows this as an empty, probably derelict, patch. The 1933 survey shows the space as a fully equipped 'Cattle Market' with a toll booth at the entrance, rows of seating, cattle pens and an auctioneer's pulpit in the centre. The porters I worked with here remembered the pulpit.

OPPOSITE: Challow station looking west in the early stages of quadrupling in 1933. The 1840 station building and the 'Gentlemen's' urinal are very similar to the arrangement at Steventon. The all-timber footbridge was erected after 1881.

The entry road to the station – and a side road to the cottages – passed by the market triangle, and on the west side of this roadway stood the 'Railway Tavern', later to be known as the 'Prince of Wales'. The tavern existed in 1840, when the local newspaper, reporting the fatal crash, referred to it as the 'Railway Tavern'. Possibly it was a coaching inn before the railway came. It stood back off the turnpike, giving enough space for carriages to draw off the road and change horses, and it had the stabling and shed to accommodate horses and carriages.

On 10 April 1835 the GWR's London Committee of Management had made an agreement with the Earl Craven of Uffington (1809–66) to build a station at Uffington. Doubtless this was the quid pro quo in return for the Earl not objecting, in Parliament, to the railway crossing his land. But with the line open to the Faringdon Road the directors reneged on the agreement: any station to serve Uffington would be in a remote location, far from any main road, whereas the Faringdon Road station occupied an excellent site alongside the Reading–Wantage–Faringdon, and Cirencester–Gloucester/

Cheltenham main road. But there was uncertainty regarding the attitude the Earl might adopt, and maybe this accounts for the Faringdon Road station being erected as a temporary building. The Board minute for 6 October 1840 states:

> Referring to the Minutes of the London Committee dated 10 April 1835, embracing the agreement with Earl Craven, and also the eligibility of constituting Faringdon Road station permanent in substitution for that originally proposed for Uffington Road. Resolved: that a negotiation be opened with the agent of Lord Craven to relinquish that part of the agreement which relates to the establishment of a depot on his property, the present Faringdon Road station being in every respect more convenient to the public and advantageous to the company. It was resolved: that subject to the cancellation of the agreement with Lord Craven so far as it relates to the Uffington Road station, a minor station to be established at Bourton on the road from Shrivenham to Bishopstone to be called 'Shrivenham station'.[2]

Faringdon Road station was more or less at the centre of the Vale and was beside a major road, so it catered for a lot of traffic. An indication of the importance the company placed on what looked like a very humble wooden wayside station is shown by the relatively high pay of its station master: £120 per annum; his clerk was paid £60, two policemen earned 16/- and 15/- respectively and a foreman porter got 21/-, but in spite of the apparent workload, there were only two porters earning 17/- and 15/- respectively. The wages staff seems to have been lacking a couple of porters, given that there was a foreman porter.

The Faringdon Road station was 5½ miles from Faringdon marketplace and 4 miles from Wantage marketplace, yet the station was named for Faringdon – the GWR clearly wanted nothing to do with Wantage, for reasons shortly to be explained.

In June 1840, a service of eight trains each way from Paddington was provided. These trains left Paddington at 8am, 9, 10, noon, 2pm, 4, 7 and 8.55pm, the last of the day being the mail. In 1840 no arrival times were given for any station along the way because the company did not trust the reliability of their engines. The single fares from Paddington to Faringdon Road were: 1st class, 14 shillings; 2nd class, 10 shillings. In summer 1841 there were nine passenger trains and two goods trains scheduled through the Vale in each direction – arrival times now shown – between about 8am and 11pm. This made a 15-hour day for one policeman, assuming the trains ran to time. This seems more likely – given the labour conditions of the period – than that two men were employed for a mere 7½ hours each.

The first fatal crash on the Great Western took place at Faringdon Road on Sunday 27 October 1840. Brunel was at the station and witnessed the event. The *Morning Chronicle* reported it thus:

> On 27 October 1840, at Faringdon Road station at 5am, the 11.15pm (Saturday) from Paddington crashed into the doors of the engine house at 15mph killing the driver, John Rose. The engine was Fire King and the fireman James James. James stated that driver Rose was a very steady, sober man to whom he had fired daily for four months. James said that when they were 1½ miles from Faringdon Road, Rose told him to put more coke on the fire and to screen it with small coke to make up the fire ready for their return journey with the 6am to Reading. That was the last time Rose spoke. James said that Rose was standing in his usual place and turned on the feed to the boiler. Rose attended to the fire and then realized that they were passing the station at about 15mph. James turned to the handbrake whilst shouting out to Rose. James screwed the handbrake on and as he was doing so the engine received a violent blow which threw him off the footplate. The engine had run into the doors of the engine house and driver Rose was killed.
>
> James said that Rose made no response when he called out and the cause of the cash was simply that Rose did not shut off steam. Driver Rose thoroughly knew his business. He and James had been working one round trip per night from Paddington, Down

and back Up again. Rose slept well during the day and he was not sleepy at the time of the crash.

Mr Brunel stated that the train approached at its normal running speed, crashed through the engine house doors smashing two wagons therein, which impact caused the two leading wagons of the train to overturn, and ran on through the end wall of the house and embedded itself in the earth. The rails did not go beyond the inside of the engine house.

This late night departure from Paddington was a goods and luggage train. There was a 3rd class passenger vehicle behind the engine's tender and behind that was a wagon loaded with planks of wood and fourteen more trucks behind that carrying, coal, goods, planks of timber and luggage in advance. Four people were riding in the 3rd class wagon and they testified to the steadiness of Rose's driving. Mr Kitchen, a dealer in earthenware, travelling home to Cheltenham from London, was thrown out of the truck and not seriously hurt but William Welling, a soap dealer from Cheltenham, Robert Edwards, a labourer from Fernham a few miles from the station, and a cattle drover returning from Brentford were seriously hurt when the planks in the wagon behind them shot forwards and hit them. The guard of the train, Mr Marlow, was riding with the passengers and was decapitated by the thrusting forward of the planks. Robert Edwards was found beneath Marlow's body when the planks were removed.

Mr Brunel sent for the local doctors, Mr Mantell of Faringdon and Mr Stayley of Wantage – a surgeon. The two dead railwaymen and the four injured passengers were carried to the Railway Tavern. Advice of the tragedy was sent to Paddington by the next Up train and later that day the Chairman of the company, Charles Russell, and the company Secretary, Charles Saunders, arrived bringing with them nurses from St George's Hospital. Driver Rose had been a driver with the GWR for two years. He was unmarried and was well known as a sober, thoroughly reliable man. Guard Marlow left a widow and two children aged 8 and 10. Charles Russell and Lord Barrington came to Faringdon to attend the Inquest held on the 29th.

Mr Stayley's bill for his work – £37 12s 6d – was authorized to be paid by the directors on 27 October 1841.[3]

A Board minute of 29 September 1841 makes surprising reading for those who knew the station:

Faringdon Road goods shed was blown down in yesterday's gale. An estimate was ordered to be prepared for restoring the same in two places, viz: two thirds of it near the Faringdon [Road] station and one third at Wootton Bassett.[4]

The choice of the word 'near' is odd – surely the rebuilt goods shed would be 'at' Faringdon Road. It is interesting to see that this timber goods shed was large enough to provide two goods sheds. I doubt whether this plan was carried out exactly as minuted: the goods shed I worked in at Challow (as Faringdon Road was known by then) was massively built in red brick, a perfect Brunel style, with huge cross-beam timbers in the vast, church-like, roof. It was more than twice the size of those provided at Wantage Road and Shrivenham, so it is surprising to find that it was not an original part of the 1840 station.

The minute of 29 October also ordered that a crossover be installed at Faringdon Road to enable Down goods trains to reverse across the Up main and into the goods shed; similar crossovers were ordered for Shrivenham and Wootton Bassett. The temporary layout of tracks at Faringdon Road when it was a terminal station is unknown, but from the minute we can tell that by September 1841 the double track extended towards Swindon and Hay Lane.

By the time the line was opened to Faringdon Road, Brunel's track, originally held down by attaching the sleepers to piles driven into the ground, had been greatly improved by cutting the sleepers free of the piles. Brunel's unstable four-wheeled passenger carriages had been replaced with six-wheelers, also designed by Brunel, which had excellent steadiness in movement. Only first-class passengers had protection from the weather.

The only other GWR vehicles that afforded their occupants complete protection from the weather were the horseboxes. They were strange wagons: 9ft 8in long but 10ft 8in wide and 7ft 6in to the roof. They ran on four 3ft-diameter wheels and the distance between the two axles was a mere 6ft. The horse or horses within would have suffered considerable terror when the train got up speed and the ultra-short wheelbase allowed the wagon to jostle and 'hunt' about.

The Great Western – Brunel's 'Gentleman's Railway' – was extremely class-conscious, just as Brunel was. Those able to pay first-class fares were accommodated in fully enclosed, well upholstered, six-wheeled carriages. These had four compartments resting on an iron frame, 24ft long. In 1841 these carriages had buffers made of horsehair stuffed into leather bags; spring-loaded buffers were fitted by 1844. Each compartment was 9ft wide and could accommodate eight passengers.[5] Each carriage weighed 7¾ tons. There was no night-time lighting in first-class compartments until, in August 1842, the directors ordered six of the seventy-eight carriages to be fitted with a roof lamp in each compartment.

Each compartment had a central door with a drop-light window and fixed panes of glass on each side of that. The wheels were 4ft in diameter. They protruded through the floor in all four compartments and were covered with a cowling – the cowlings partly obstructed the doorways of the two end compartments, frequently causing an unwary passenger to make an inelegant exit onto the platform.

Those who could not afford first-class fares were accommodated in six-wheeled second-class vehicles. These were 20ft 9in long, 8ft 6in wide and 6ft 9in from floor to roof. They weighed 7¼ tons and had sprung buffers. There was room for sixty people in six compartments sitting on transverse planks, including the train guard sitting at his screw-down brake handle.[6] The wooden sides of the carriage rose halfway up the distance from floor to roof, but above that they were open to the elements. They too had 4ft wheels under cowlings

that encroached sufficiently into the doorways to be a hazard.

Passengers died of exposure when travelling long distances in what a doctor, in a letter to *The Times* in 1844, referred to as 'these barbarous structures'.[7] E.T. McDermott states that these 'open seconds' had all been withdrawn from service, or had glass fitted into the open sides, by the end of 1844, but that is not true. In January 1845 a man was found in a second-class carriage in Bath frozen to the point of death. He was carried outside the station and dumped on the pavement, where he died.[8] Letters to *The Times* as late as 20 March 1845 prove that death from exposure occurred in GWR second-class carriages. These carriages may or may not have been glazed by then, but the bare interior without even cushions to warm the backside was grim and potentially fatal in winter. The general consensus of public opinion, as expressed in the newspapers of the time, was that these carriages were designed to force as many as possible to buy the first-class fare.

Third-class passengers travelled in an open truck closely resembling a coal wagon with plank seats; the company called these 'Common waggons'. They were four-wheelers, with solid wood projections at each end of the frames to do duty as buffers. Their wooden sides rose only 2ft above the floor, while the plank seats lifted the passengers 18in from the floor, so for all practical purposes passengers were carried without side walls to stop them falling off when the wagon was jerked and tugged about during starting or stopping, or when they jostled from side to side when the speed rose above 30mph. The fare to Faringdon Road from Paddington in one of these was for 6/-, and 14lb of luggage could be carried free of charge.

The Regulation of Railways Act of 9 August 1844 laid a legal obligation on all railway companies to provide enclosed carriages for third-class passengers, and that at least one train a day in each direction should be run, at a speed not less than 12mph including stops, at a fare of one penny per mile – these were the 'Parliamentary' trains.

In September 1845 the GWR brought out their improved carriages for the third class. They looked like vans to transport convicts. They had a body 26ft 8in long, made of thin sheets of wrought iron on a wooden framing, with sprung buffers and small windows at the eaves level in each of the seven doors. The seating remained transverse wooden planks 18in above the floor, but each plank had a low back for the impecunious traveller to rest against until that became unbearable and he or she had to sit up straight. At night a single oil lamp, placed in the roof at the centre, shed the dimmest of light on the gruesome scene. These vehicles became guard's brake vans in 1860 as the company began to learn its business and provided relatively civilized carriages for third-class passengers.

Trains ran at up to 60mph with minimal brakes. There was no brake at all on the engine, but there was a screw-down handbrake on the tender. The second- and – from 1845 – third-class carriages were equipped with a relatively powerful handbrake operated by the train guard, applying brake blocks to all six wheels.

The safety of any railway is a matter of keeping trains apart. The railway had opened in 1838 from Paddington to the twenty-second mile post, but it was not until 1840 that there were any signals other than the hand signals of lineside policemen. In 1840 Brunel designed the 'disc and crossbar' signal. In the absence of powerful brakes, Brunel's idea was to make the signals visible from as far away as possible to give drivers the best chance of stopping at a 'danger' signal. The disc was 4ft in diameter and the crossbar 8ft long by 15in deep; they were fixed together, the disc above the crossbar and at 90 degrees to it. The disc and the crossbar were painted bright red and were mounted on a pole between 40ft and 60ft tall, which was turned by the station policeman. There was, initially, only one signal to apply to both the Up and the Down lines.

When the disc was facing the train, the driver understood that the line was clear ahead and when the crossbar was showing – the disc would then be edgeways-on and almost invisible – 'danger – Stop' was indicated. After a train had passed, the crossbar was turned on for three minutes and then the disc was turned on. Should a train approach within

the next seven minutes the policeman would give the driver a 'caution' signal with his arm. At night a white light was hoisted to indicate 'All right' and a Red light for 'danger'. The night hoisted signals had powerful oil lamps visible in clear weather for 5 miles where the line was straight enough – such as at Twyford. The 'caution' signal at night would have been a green light held by the policeman. Hence the little saying, 110 years old, when I was given it by the Challow signalman in 1953: 'White is Right and Red is Wrong – Green means Gently Go Along.'

In 1841 the Board of Trade carried out experiments in braking on the Eastern Counties Railway.[9] The result was that a train – weight not given – travelling at 30mph on a dry rail could be stopped in 15 seconds, by which time it had travelled 65yd. When the rails were wet, 180yd was needed to stop. The stop was achieved by the driver putting the engine into reverse while the fireman screwed down the handbrake on the tender and the guard – in answer to the driver's steam whistle – screwed down his brake. This remained the only way of stopping until the gradual introduction of a powered brake from 1876 onwards.

Riding the footplate of his cabless engine, the driver had no protection from the weather. His eyes watering in the slipstream of speed at 50mph or more, he had less and less chance of seeing the signal from a distance that would enable him to stop at it, especially in fog, heavy rain, cold or falling snow. The 'time interval' did not guarantee that the line ahead was clear to the next 'Stop' signal because a train could break down and be stationary out of sight of the policeman it had passed. To guard against rear-end collisions the Great Western introduced 'exploding warning devices' in a minute dated 26 October 1848.[10] These were the famous 'detonators', carried by the guard of the train. Should his train stop between stations, he would walk back ¾mile and clip three detonators, 10yd apart, to the crown.

The Great Western was the first railway in the world to use the electric telegraph. It was installed between West Drayton and Paddington in 1838, renewed on an improved system and extended to Slough in 1843. The directors did not appreciate the huge importance to railway operations of the telegraph. Brunel did not persuade them otherwise, and it was abandoned June 1849.

In January 1842 Brunel designed an extra signal to stand beside the disc and crossbar. The new signal consisted of a broad, deep board, which was pointed at one end and had a 'fishtail' cut in the other end. It was mounted on a shorter pole than the disc and crossbar. When the crossbar was showing, the pointed end of the board was nearest the track, showing its red face to the driver; after three minutes it was turned 180 degrees to show the green face, indicating 'caution'. After seven minutes, it was turned edgeways on to the train. Also in 1842, Brunel hit on the clever idea of having separate signals for the Up Down lines and Brunel modified his cumbersome signals. He put the disc and crossbar on top of a metal rod which ran through eyelets screwed into a wooden supporting post. This made the job of turning the signal very much easier.

But still the station policemen had a terrible job, working twelve or fifteen hours each day or night, six days a week, walking many miles back and forth to attend to the signals and switches in all the seasons, in any kind of weather. There was no advance communication and if a policeman had a watch he bought it himself. He knew more or less when a train was supposed to appear but once that time passed he had no idea when it might turn up. This made his job at level crossings or at stations impossible to carry out safely. When a cart wanted to cross the line or a porter wanted to put a wagon out on the main line the policeman just had to hold up road traffic or stop the porter's work until the errant train passed – or take a chance and let a wagon be placed on the main line, or open the gates and allow the cart across.

Six to eight men a year, out of the whole regiment of Great Western police- and switchmen, managed to earn the £5 yearly bonus for working without being reported for any cause whatsoever – they were exceptionally lucky men. Many more were

reported for breaking the rules, most commonly for being asleep at his post or for deserting his post to go to the pub, or simply being absent when the inspector turned up. All transgressors of the company's rules were summoned to appear before the directors at Paddington.

Constable Clewitt at Faringdon Road was summoned on 4 December 1845 charged with 'having the red signal on as the train passed the station'. As written in the minute there was no crime, but what the minute meant to say was that he had not changed the signal from red to white after the passing of the previous train – the implication being that he had gone to sleep. He was 'cautioned' for the future and fined five shillings to be paid in two instalments.[11] This incident is also interesting because the minute does not say that Clewitt's failure had caused unnecessary delay, and there is no mention of the driver of that train being hauled up before the directors for ignoring the red signal.

GWR passenger engines' tenders had a seat at the rearmost corner of the tender. The seat had a tall back and sides to shelter the 'travelling porter' who sat there, facing the carriages, enclosed by the walls of the 'iron coffin'. There was a platform across the back of the tender, just above the buffers, across which the travelling porter was supposed to walk while the train was at speed so that he could keep a look out on both sides of the train for 'signals of alarm'. These men, in winter, frequently had to be lifted out, chilled to the bone, unable to stand, and be carried to somewhere warm to thaw out. There were occasions when their clothing was frozen to the iron sides and they had to be cut out of the seat.

In mid-January 1848 a passenger train had just left Steventon and was accelerating when a second-class carriage began to rock and shake violently. The passengers creaked to their feet in the icy slip-stream and yelled, hollered and waved towards the travelling porter. There was no response from him for over ten minutes until, approaching Faringdon Road, he woke up and yelled to his driver to stop. Upon examination, the flanged tyre of a wheel on the second-class coach had come away from the wheel.[12]

The Devizes & Wiltshire Gazette for 1 October 1846 reported a derailment at Faringdon Road caused by the clumsy method drivers had to adopt to stop their train. On Monday 28 September 1846 the superintendent of Faringdon Road station, Henry Stevens, was on the Down platform waiting for the arrival of a passenger train. The name of the train was not recorded but the driver was Robert Patterson. Stevens is quoted as saying:

I head a crash as the train got to the bridge. I immediately ran towards the bridge and saw fire flying out from each side of the train and saw that the luggage van was raised onto the first passenger carriage. The engine parted from the train and ran forwards.

The luggage van had four wheels and with the exception of its internal partitions is made of iron. The passenger carriage which goes next to the van has a wooden body. The luggage van contained nineteen boxes of gold bullion weighing 15cwt. There was also passengers' luggage. I heard the crash and as the train came near the platform there was another check when the luggage van which was derailed hit the [barrow] crossing at the platform and this forced the passenger carriage further into the van.

GWR Police Constable Robert Matthews, No. 395, stated:

I was walking under the bridge along the platform to go to the signal post which was on the other side. I was enveloped in fire and smoke and dust and did not know what was happening. I groped my way to the signal post and remained there as the train passed.

Mr Thomas Bush, an engineer, part owner of the engineering company Bush & Beddoe of Bristol, was asked to investigate for the GWR:

The most likely cause was the breaking of the coupling between the luggage van and the locomotive tender after steam was shut off and braking was taking place. The luggage van ran heavily into the tender, rebounded, broke the coupling, ran forwards hard against the braking engine and was thrown upwards to knock a lump out of the brick arch.

Faringdon Road became 'Challow' in June 1864 when the Uffington–Faringdon branch railway opened.

Faringdon passenger/parcels statistics[6]

Year	No. of staff	Annual wage cost £	Total income of station £	Tickets sold	Season tickets
1903	7	515	15678	18056	nil
1913	9	741	17667	19023	nil
1923	11	1783	27537	14051	5
1929	10	1717	21704	9281	14
1930	11	1760	21690	8168	18
1933	8	1457	11036	4569	6
1938	8	1273	19829	1445	2

CHAPTER 4

Wantage Road

This town – birthplace of King Alfred the Great, no less – was known as 'Black Wantage' up to the mid-19th century and had a frightful reputation as the refuge of murderers and thieves escaping from the law in London. There were few visitors, the most regular being the Bow Street runners, who would always come to Wantage when searching for a seriously bad criminal. It is very likely that the gentlemanly and aristocratic directors of the GWR had no wish to advertise an association with the place, nor provide nefarious persons with even faster means of escaping justice. This is why the Faringdon Road station – two miles closer to Wantage than Faringdon – was named after the more distant but much more law-abiding place.

The *Reading Mercury* for 16 September 1843 reported that the Wantage Agricultural Association had 'complained bitterly' – presumably to the turnpike trustees – of 'the atrocious state of the road between the Faringdon Road station and Wantage'. On 23 January 1845, a leading Wantage resident, the lawyer George Ormond, asked the GPO (post office) for a mid-day delivery and for a late afternoon deadline for getting letters into the mail system. The GPO declined.

George Ormond and William Trinder, a governor of Wantage Townlands, were the pioneers of attempts to improve Wantage. Both of them are commemorated in the names of roads: Ormond being an appropriately important thoroughfare and Trinder a lane leading into Ormond. In 1847 Charles Hart opened the Wantage Engineering Company with a foundry and machine shops to build very fine steam road locomotives. The only time a clergyman came to the town was to collect his tithes, until, in 1849, the Revd Butler took up residence as vicar and began his successful work of encouraging the people to rouse themselves – and indeed, even to wash themselves, apparently.[1]

In 1845, Ormond and Trinder went to see the directors of the Great Western Railway. The directors' minutes for 10 April 1845, page 66, record in Olympian fashion:

A deputation from the town of Wantage with Mr Ormond – a lawyer of that place – attended the directors in support of the Prayer of certain memorials recently received, that the directors would construct a station at the Grove Road as most convenient for the town of Wantage and neighbourhood. After hearing the arguments brought forward by the Deputation and referring to the Ordnance maps of the County the Chairman acquainted them with the Board's resolve that a siding and a shed be constructed as an experiment to ascertain whether the trade in goods or in cattle will be remunerative – and that the Luggage train be permitted to call at Grove on two or three days a week.[2]

The railway was about 1½ miles north of the village of Grove and 2½ miles north of Wantage. A goods station was created consisting of a small goods shed on the open space on the south side of the line, and the east side of the bridge connected to the Down main line by a siding. No diagram exists, so we do not know if there was a crossover to enable Up goods trains to get into the siding.

The GWR two-chain survey of 1875 shows a 'Tavern' at the entrance to the goods yard convenient for the toll keeper's cottage and the toll bar.

On 12 July 1846, William Trinder wrote to the GWR directors 'requesting that the 10.15 Down train and the 4pm Up might stop at Grove'. It is significant that the 'station' was referred to as 'Grove', not Wantage Road. As this was a goods station the Up and Down 'Parliamentary' trains were not obliged to stop here, but as a favour to the town one Up and one Down 'Parliamentary' called. Passengers had to climb aboard from rail level. A horse and carriage plied to and fro between Wantage and Faringdon Road station to meet all passenger trains.

On 13 October 1849 the *Reading Mercury* reported that:

> Every train will stop at Faringdon Road on 25 October to permit people to go to the celebrations in Wantage for the 800th anniversary of the birth of King Alfred. A general holiday has been announced.

Wantage pestered Paddington with requests for improvement. The *Reading Mercury* for 6 March 1858 reported a petition to Paddington to stop, on Wednesdays only, the 11.57am Up from Faringdon Road and the 3.34pm Down at Faringdon Road; these were needed for the convenience of people coming and going to Wantage market. They also requested the 8.55am Up from Swindon and the 4.45pm Down from Paddington. The petition was ignored.

Colonel Lloyd-Lindsay (1832–1901), returning to Wantage from the Crimean War in 1855 with a Victoria Cross, threw himself and his national reputation into the fray by bringing Wantage into the

orderliness and employment of the second half of the 19th century. He had money, and he spent it on doing nothing but good for Wantage and Berkshire; he became Lord Wantage in 1885. In June 1862 the townspeople signed a petition for better passenger accommodation at Wantage Road. The GWR ignored that.

Early in August 1863 – when the train service at Wantage Road station consisted of a goods from Gloucester calling at 7.30am, the only Up passenger train calling at 4.5pm and a Down passenger train calling at 10.53am – Mr Ormond sent another petition to the GWR directors asking for 'a passenger station to serve Wantage at the Grove site'. His request was considered by the directors on 20 August: they resolved to postpone a decision for further thought. They knew that the branch line from a new station called Uffington – at the 66½ mile post – to Faringdon would open in 1864; maybe this would enable them to close the Faringdon Road station and then perhaps they would build the passenger station for Wantage.[3] A very strong protest from Faringdon, against the closure of Faringdon Road made them change their minds.

A few weeks later Ormond asked the GWR for a policeman to supervise the level crossing of the railway by a lane from Grove to Hanney about half a mile west of the goods station at Wantage Road.[4] This shows that the GWR was content to leave even well-used crossings unattended in those early days.

The 1863 list of staff at the Wantage station proves that it was still a goods station. There were: a clerk for the goods traffic, paid 30/- a week; two policemen, paid 19 and 15/- respectively; and one porter paid 19/-.[5]

On Tuesday 23 May 1864 a deputation went to see the chairman of the Great Western, Richard Potter, at Paddington. Chief amongst the deputation was one of the most powerful men in Britain, the banker Lord Overstone. With him came his son-in-law, Colonel Lloyd-Lindsay, George Ormond and five others. They urged upon the chairman the necessity of improving facilities for passengers at Wantage Road. Confronted by the leading banker and economist in England and the illustrious colonel, the GWR chairman became obsequious to the point of exaggeration. Mr Potter informed them that the company was already erecting platforms and that the timetable for June would show the improvements. He emphasized the company's faith in Wantage Road by stating that the directors were considering the closure of Faringdon Road station when the Faringdon branch line opened in a week's time. Potter knew that both of those statements were incorrect – and so did the deputation.

A minute of the GWR directors' Expenditure Committee, dated 7 June 1865, states:

> Further to Board Minute No. 12 of 5 January 1865 a circular letter was sent out to various contractors asking for their tenders for building the station and platforms at Wantage Road. Three have now been received: Evan & Co, £1,450; George Drew, £1,139 and Henry Lovatt, £1,065. Mr Lovatt's tender has been accepted.[6]

Judging from the foregoing, the passenger station at Wantage Road was probably opened to the public late in 1865. On 12 December 1865 a meeting was held in Wantage to summon investment in a broad gauge branch line into Wantage town from the main line. The promoters of this project cheerfully believed that the GWR would provide the locomotives and rolling stock.[7] Nothing came of this.

The station of 1865 was three storeys tall, in red brick, with a low-pitched, slated roof. It was built on the south (Down) side of the line, west of the road bridge but so close to the bridge that the bridge parapet merged with the wall of the station house. The original design had the entrance to the booking hall at road level with a canopy sheltering it. Once inside, the public space in front of the booking office window was cramped and gloomy. The station master's living quarters were on the second floor with stairs leading up from the booking office space. For the public, narrow and steep stairs led down to the platform with waiting rooms and lavatories. There was also a passageway through the bridge from the Down platform to the goods yard for the convenience of railway staff.

The station was supplied with a horse to move goods wagons and to pump water. This is clear from a report in the *Reading Mercury* of 20 April 1867 concerning the death of William Ireson. Ireson owned the horse and handled it for all work. Helping Ireson was GWR porter Henry Wilkins.

Wilkins stated at Ireson's inquest that they were pulling wagons along the siding next to the Down main, the horse and Ireson being in the Down main. Having got a wagon rolling, the chain was uncoupled so that the wagon could roll on into the goods shed to stand near the points leading to the Down main, to go out on the Down goods at 5.30pm. Ireson would turn the horse and go back, walking in the Down main, to couple to the next one standing on the siding. Why he could not have walked on the gravel between the two tracks is a mystery. Wilkins said that 'the horse was old and stiff in his joints and turned with difficulty'. As Ireson had got the horse broadside-on right across the Down main, an

Wantage Road station, looking east on the Up platform, c. 1955. LENS OF SUTTON

Wantage Road looking east from the Down side, c. 1955. R.M. CASSERLEY

express train appeared ¼ mile – 20 seconds – away. Ireson tried to get the horse to back up and tried to turn him but the horse could not be rushed. Ireson was still pushing and shoving when the locomotive hit them. Both were killed instantly. The inquest jury returned a verdict of accidental death. The Iresons were a popular family and a communal 'whip-round' was made which raised enough for William Ireson's eldest son to buy a horse and take over his father's job at the station.

On 29 July 1869 a royal train came from Windsor to Wantage Road station carrying the Prince and Princess Christian for a visit to Colonel and Mrs Lloyd-Lindsay at Lockinge House. The princess was the fifth child of Queen Victoria and until she married the Prince of Schleswig-Holstein was known as Princess Helena. She, like Lloyd-Lindsay, was a tireless organizer of good works and among other feats, she was, with Lloyd-Lindsay, the founder of the Red Cross in 1870 in response to the outbreak of the Franco-Prussian War.

A standard gauge roadside tramway was built from the station to the town and was opened for goods traffic and for passengers on 1 and 11 October 1875, respectively. A tramway is a different legal entity from a railway, is much cheaper to build and operate, and is very much slower. A tramway requires no signalling and no train staff, although there were passing loops proving that two trams were allowed to approach each other on the single track. It was built with bullhead rails on cross-sleepered track. All the vehicles were horse-drawn at first.

The track from the station divided at the foot of the hill into the town, the right-hand branch continuing more or less on level ground to the goods terminus 100yd from Wantage Mill at the bottom of Mill Street, while the 'main line' went up the hill to the passenger terminus near the top of Mill Street. The terminus was a single platform sheltered by a pitched, slated roof.

The Wantage Tramway Company was very progressive. They allowed John Grantham to experiment with a steam-engined tram car during 1875 and on 1 August 1876 this entered service, making the rural Wantage tramway the first steam-hauled tramway in the world. Locomotive engines were later added to the haulage.

The *Berkshire Chronicle* for 10 November 1876 carried this report:

No. 5, affectionately 'Jane' but officially un-named, stopped for the benefit of Jack Hollick. There was no turntable and No. 5 always ran with its chimney facing Wantage Road station. The train, travelling towards Wantage, was photographed between the Grove village turn and the goods/passenger station junction, c.1925. DR JACK HOLLICK/AUTHOR

On Saturday last the goods engine of the Wantage tram came out of the goods line exactly in time to collide with the Grantham steam car going to meet the 1.6pm arrival at Wantage Road station. Some persons within the car were bruised but Mr J.H. Harris, sitting on the roof [sic – the journalist meant 'outside on the top deck'] fell and his injuries have confined him to bed.

At the railway station end the tram track ran alongside the base of the rising embankment of the road, crossing the railway. There was a run-round loop for the engine and a siding connecting the tramway with the railway goods sidings.

After the Wantage tramway was opened, most passengers to and from the town arrived at the station by tram; the GWR therefore built a booking office at platform level in time for the opening of the tramway. What had been the booking office – reached from the main road rising over the railway – was converted to extra space for the station master and his family. Passengers getting off the tram simply walked through the southern side arch of the bridge and onto the Down platform for the booking office. Passengers arriving off an Up train had no footbridge on which to cross the line until quadrupling in 1932: they walked through the north-side arch and crossed the track on the barrow crossing.

Starting in the June to December timetable of 1879, the 9am Paddington to Kingswear – a broad gauge train until May 1892 – conveyed a slip coach at the rear for Wantage. There was a guard in the slip coach who pulled the lever to uncouple the coach from the train, about ¾ mile before the station, and then to bring the vehicle to a stand at the platform at 10.30am as the rest of the train went through at about 55mph. This was a daily event, always with the same train, until December 1914. The coach had then to be immediately drawn back off the Down main and placed on the siding. The 1879 timetable gives no indication as to how this was done. An engine might have been specially sent from Didcot as it is unlikely that the shunting horse could have moved it. The 1910 timetable shows the 9.35am Didcot to Swindon goods train waiting in the goods yard, the engine of which would have been used to retrieve the coach and attach to the goods train: it arrived at Swindon around mid-day and was attached to a Didcot-bound train as an ordinary coach.[8]

In May 1888 the Board of Trade appears to have received a complaint from Wantage concerning the accommodation for passengers at the station. Colonel Rich was sent to inspect and made a report to the Board of Trade, which is not in GWR records. Mr Voss, of the Chief Civil Engineer's Office at Reading, was ordered to inspect the station and

Wantage Road goods yard, c. 1955. The tramway ran up to where the City of Oxford Motor Bus Co. bus is standing. The transfer siding, now cut short, is on the right. R.M. CASSERLEY

report on the colonel's observations. Voss's report is dated 19 June and politely demolishes the Colonel:

Report on the suggestions made by Colonel Rich in his report to the Board of Trade of 11 May

Colonel Rich suggests 'that the old booking office on the road should be re-established' and the present booking office 'should be appropriated as a waiting room'. As will be seen from the enclosed plan of the station, there is at present a general waiting room as well as a ladies' room on the Down side affording ample accommodation for passengers at this small station. This escaped Colonel Rich's attention. Nearly all the passengers come to the station by the tramway and are deposited close to the side arch on the low level, Down side. If the booking office were on the high level they would have to go out of the yard, cross the road and up the slope to get their tickets and down the staircase to the platform instead of going through the arch to the booking office on the down platform.

As to the bridge. It was built in 1839. A settlement of about two inches on the east side of the centre arch over the down line took place when the centres were removed but it has gone no further since. Mr Owen, the late Chief Engineer, made a careful examination of the bridge with me shortly after it came under my charge in 1868. We came to the conclusion that the bridge was perfectly safe although the arch was crippled and unsightly. It was decided to lay a thin layer of cement over the crack so that any further settlement could easily be detected. No further movement has taken place.

As to his statement that 'the brickwork of the arch at the Down side of the line has been drawn about three inches apart'. This is not so. There are some holes in the soffit of the arch where the telegraph insulators have been fixed and removed but this does not affect the stability of the arch.

The appearance of the bridge would be improved by pointing: a proper footpath through the small archway on the Down side would be a convenience; it would also be desirable to take down and rebuild the east side parapet as Colonel Rich suggests.[9]

In 1924 the Great Western inaugurated a road motor bus service serving Wantage and district. The passenger service on the tramway was withdrawn in 1925 but goods traffic continued until 21 December 1945; there was a suspension between November 1943 and February 1944 owing to damage done to the tracks by vehicles, US Army and others, constructing Grove aerodrome. The GWR directors agreed to cosmetically restore the 0–4–0 tank engine No. 5 'Shannon' – usually known as 'Jane' – and place it on display, under a canopy, close to the booking office and waiting room on the Down platform at Wantage Road. This was done in April 1948.

The British economy began to expand in 1933 and in 1935 it grew by 4 per cent, but the revenue of the GWR grew by only 1 per cent and indeed, all the the wayside railway stations went the other way.[10]

During the Second World War the railways were again in great demand, and without the hard labour and expertise of the railwaymen the war would not have gone on as well as it did. In spite of hunger due to rationing, working for days at a time without going home, no footplateman struck work, nor indeed did any other railwayman or -woman. After the First World War and the various strikes culminating in the General Strike of 1926, railwaymen did not go on strike again until 1955.

The railway was vital for the transporting of men and stores, ambulance trains, petrol, guns and bombs. Wantage Road received the building materials for the American air base at Grove: the navvies, many of them Irish, who built it; the USAAF personnel who ran it; and the supplies for the base once it had become operational. This took place on 1 December 1943 when it became part of the US 9 Air Force. Wantage Road's sidings would have been full of wagons for the town and locality, for Grove air base and for the military stores depot at Lockinge. Wantage porters would have worked hard for their pay.

After the war, traffic declined only slowly at first, owing to petrol rationing and the shortage of road freight transport. But fall off it did, until the station was closed for all purposes on 5 December 1964.

Wantage Road porter Sam Loder, a good friend of the author who served in the Grenadier Guards 1930–45, c. 1955. DAVID CASTLE

Wantage Road passenger/parcels statistics[11]

Year	No. of staff	Annual wage cost £	Total income of station £	Tickets sold	Season tickets	Goods £
1903	17	1029	21402	27955	nil	11885
1913	15	890	24385	30607	nil	14238
1923	14	2524	32459	33039	26	18730
1929	17	2859	25444	18514	13	15481
1930	16	2816	24260	16548	24	14039
1933	12	2217	15139	11764	9	9831
1938	12	2185	11262	9644	17	7986

CHAPTER 5

Challow

Faringdon Road station was re-named Challow with the opening of the Faringdon branch railway from Uffington, on 1 June 1864.

There had never been well water at the Faringdon Road/Challow station. Wells had been sunk but the water was always undrinkable – indeed, Challow water was not considered suitable for locomotive boilers. So it was that a broad gauge wagon carrying a tank for drinking water had ferried back and forth between the station and Kemble ever since the opening of the railway thereto – Kemble water was very pure.[1] But with the abolition of the broad gauge on the Gloucester line beyond Swindon in February 1872, the broad gauge Challow water tank had to be filled at Swindon, and the water that it brought back was unfit to drink. Challow's station master complained to the superintendent of the line, Mr Tyrrell, and on 29 June 1872 Tyrrell wrote to the Locomotive Carriage & Wagon Superintendent at Swindon, Joseph Armstrong:

> I am informed that [the Challow water tank] has been returned to Swindon and that the water contained in it has not been fit to drink recently. Please have the tank transferred to a narrow gauge truck in order that it may go to Kemble by the Gloster goods as before.

Such a mundane item as a water tank was like a leaf on the forest floor in the vastness, the rush and roar,

of Swindon Works. On 11 July Tyrrell wrote asking Armstrong, who was busy designing locomotives, to have the tank converted and returned to Challow 'as they are in need of it'.

Armstrong sent this to the carriage and wagon works manager, Thomas Clayton, having scribbled across the letter 'Kindly do the necessary'.

Clayton was supervising the erection of new carriage works and was far too busy to be bothered. On 22 July, the divisional superintendent at Reading wrote to Joseph Armstrong asking for the tank to be returned 'at once as the station people are drinking rain water.' On this terse note is written: 'Mr Clayton says it will be sent in a few days. Waiting for an old wagon to load it on.'

On 7 August the tank had not returned to Challow. This then produced another urgent note from G.N. Tyrrell to Joseph Armstrong. That went through to someone called Griffin, who wrote to Clayton on the 9th:

> Challow water tank No. 169. The above is transshipped from a B.G. carriage truck to No. 169 N.G. [narrow gauge – GWR-speak for 'standard gauge'] wagon and will be put in traffic today.

The station received the tank off the 'Gloster goods' on the 10th. And there the story ends until 13 November 1885, when the tank started to leak. Considering that this had carried water since about 1840, it had given good service. The tank was returned to Swindon for repairs or replacement, and a chain of events similar to that related above then ensued. The station remained reliant upon the water tank wagon for drinking water at least until 1934, judging by a photograph from that year.

Country stations became embedded in their district, the station master having a status similar to that of the local doctor, clergyman or post master, and the station staff were respected men. The country station gave considerable employment to the local men and at higher wages than they would receive on the farms around the place. The village station was more important to the district than the village church. 'You may Telegraph from here' said the blue and white enamelled sign. It was where excursion trains carried passengers off to 'the football' at Swindon or Reading or even to the seaside – Weston-super-Mare or even Weymouth – and at a cheap rate.

Challow station was all of this and more: it was a little village of its own. The row of railway staff cottages with their families and their gardens in front and behind, the 'Prince of Wales' beside the busy road, and the market ground drawing regular crowds by road and rail, all made it a cheerful,

populous place. Opposite the pub, across the road, was Petwick Farm and half a mile west of the station, just north of the line, was Northfield Farm; 150yd south of the line, just west of the signal box, was Petwick Cottage, a two-storey redbrick house and, beyond that, South Farm. There were, in fact, lots of working people in the vicinity of the station and the place was a village community underpinned by the life-long employment of working for the railway.

The station master from around 1920 until 1944–45 was Mr Gardiner. He lived with his wife in the company's well-made house at the end of the terrace of staff cottages. Mr and Mrs Gardiner felt the need to live up to the importance and the responsibility of being a station master. After the 'grouping' in 1923 – when the GWR was forced by the Railways Act of 1921 to take over and restore sixty impecunious railway companies – scores of antique railway carriages were hauled to Swindon to be broken up. The GWR had to build replacements, which of course the company, not the government, had to pay for. So there were then lots of carriage bodies for sale. Mr Gardiner bought a mid-Victorian, North London Railway carriage that had been sold as worn out by that company to the

The chapel coach, in a sad state, in 1984. Mr Gardiner's bungalow roof is visible behind.

Cleobury Mortimer & Ditton Priors Light Railway and now, decades later, was absorbed into the Great Western.

The carriage was delivered to the station and with great ingenuity was carried from the wagon in the unloading dock to a site in the allotments which lay just south of the staff terraced housing. Mr and Mrs Gardiner painted suitable religious exhortations all along the inside of the coach, above the windows, and brought in a harmonium and pews. For the next twenty years Sunday worship was conducted here, by Mr Gardiner and preachers on the local Methodist circuit. In the afternoon his wife took the Sunday school class. The author's friend Jim Brown, who was born at Petwick Cottage in 1932, says it was 'almost obligatory' for the children of the neighbourhood to attend.

Other staff members from 1920 onwards included Harry Strong and Albert Stanley. Albert and Harry came to Challow in the early 1920s – Harry was the porter in charge of the shunting horse, 'Duchess'. She had a stable attached to the west end of the goods shed. Both men were working at Challow when it closed in December 1964. Albert lived in the station terrace with his wife and family, but Harry cycled in from his cottage on the main road in Standford-in-the-Vale.

During the war Albert and Harry carried out Olympic feats of work and cycling, but no medal did they receive. They could be booked to work at Steventon or anywhere in the Swindon district. In the decades before the war Albert had worked at Marlborough station for the week of Marlborough's 'Mop' hiring and sheep fair. He was also rostered to work at the North Savernake ammunition depot during the Second World War for loading and unloading. To be there for 8am he cycled to Swindon and there caught a train; coming home, he could get a train from one of the two Savernake stations back to Challow.

The 1840-built station never had a station garden in the usual way but, on the west-facing bank, on the Up side, beside the 1840 bridge, a very inventive decorative advert for the Great Western was formed with whitewashed stones. It read:

Cornwall
Has
Attractive
Landscapes
Looe &
Other
Watering places
Go **W**estern **R**oute

To the left of that, planted in the platform on a short post, with the brick abutment of the bridge behind it, was the handsome wooden post Up starting signal with the signal for the Up goods loop bracketed out to the left.

During 1932 and 1933 the 1840 station was demolished and a plain red-brick station office was erected a few yards to the east on the same side of the line as part of the quadrupling of the line. The tracks ran in a shallow cutting through ordinary soil, giving no difficulty to excavation. The old Up and Down main lines became the Up relief and Up main, and two new tracks were added on the Down side. The ancient layout of sidings and their connections with the old Up main, now Up relief, line remained unaltered. The broad gauge brick arch spanning the double track had to be replaced by a steel girder bridge spanning the four tracks and both platforms. The platforms were extended below the bridge and were long enough for a twelve-coach train. A steel-plate bridge was erected to carry the A417 road over the platforms and four tracks.

So as not to close the main road, the old arch was cut in half lengthways. There was a parapet on one side and nothing at all on the other. Road traffic, which of course was a great deal less than it is today, crossed the railway on the half a road's width. Traction engines hauling threshing tackle went across, the hubs of the engine's wheels missing the parapet and the unprotected drop on the tracks on the other side by an inch.

One day during these works William Hutt – of whom more later – was driving a horse and wagon over this bridge. Down below on the tracks, men were working on laying additional track and building platforms. Engine drivers would blow

Looking east past the GWR Type 1 signal box.

1933: looking east off the old footbridge with the foundations for the new station office in preparation.

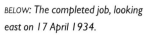

BELOW: The completed job, looking east on 17 April 1934.

their steam whistle as they approached to warn the track workers. The horse was unhappy about the narrowness of the bridge and the gap down to the track on one side. When a steam whistle blew close to the bridge, this was too much: the horse bolted violently, throwing Hutt off his seat, to the right, onto the road. His coat caught on a wheel hub of the cart and he was dragged along, pressed against the brick parapet: he was very badly injured. The workmen went across to the five-bar gate at the Down side entrance road, took the gate off its hinges, placed William's body on it and carried him to his close-by home, Petwick Cottage.

Jim Hutt became a porter at Challow in 1939. He had been the 'chicken boy' at nearby Northfield Farm. He was called up, aged twenty, and was put into the Royal Electrical & Mechanical Engineers and served in the Western Desert and Italy. Ronald Rowland became a Challow porter just before the war, was called up and became a 'Chindit' in Burma. The very important 'lamp man', well before 1939, was Harold Titchener who lived in one of the railway houses; he was still looking after the signal lamps at Challow, Wantage Road and Steventon in 1964. The track was maintained by a gang of six men. Before the war the ganger was Butty Martin, who was ganger at Uffington in the 1950s and early 1960s, with Bob Thatcher as ganger at Challow.

The signalmen at Challow in 1939 were Bert Snell, Bill Windridge and Bert Winter. The station became more heavily used during the war, with Irish navvies arriving to build the airfields at Shellingford and Grove and living in the area. US and British servicemen used the station, and prisoners of war were de-trained here for local camps – there were Italian prisoners at East Challow. Traffic for Grove and Shellingford and also a military depot at Challow made life hectic for the porters, so extra staff were recruited. There were four female porters at Challow during the war: Barbara Comely, Dorothy Ayres, Miss Taylor and Flossie Barnes.

Jim Brown was born in 1932 at Petwick Cottage, which had been his grandparents' house. His grandfather, William Hutt, earned his living as a small farmer, butcher and general labourer. Jim's father worked at Northfield Farm. Jim grew up at the station and in the fields around the place, and has never lived further than ten miles from the station. In his book *Jim Brown Remembers a Wartime Boyhood in the Vale of the White Horse*, Jim conveys beautifully the remoteness of the place and the importance of the station both to small boys and to the district at large. Small boys were surely a sore trial to Mr Gardiner: supposedly he told them off, but clearly not sufficiently to ban them from the station. With Jim's permission I can quote from his writing:

No-one travelled far in those days. My mother used to go shopping in Wantage and occasionally we went to Faringdon, but past there was unknown territory to us. I can remember going to Swindon because you could get cheap day returns from Challow station. The head carter on the farm was a keen Reading supporter and he would go if he could. If my father was feeling a bit free with money he would sometimes take me on the train to Reading for the football. The big city was like a foreign country to me – even the people seemed strange. We only knew what was within our domain, which was limited by how far you could walk or cycle. There was a Fry's Chocolate dispensing machine – one penny in the slot – in the waiting room. Me and my older brother used to put a halfpenny coin on the rail and when it had been rolled over by an engine it became the size of a full penny. But when pushed into the machine it usually jammed. But that didn't stop us trying. We were given a pair of second-hand roller skates and we took them to the station to practise with on he platform, but Mr Gardiner chased us off.

When the war came, gas masks were issued to everyone and Mr Gardiner volunteered the station's waiting room as the place of issue of gas masks to all living nearby. He and his wife handed out the masks and paid particular attention to the children, putting them on each child in turn, and making sure they were a good fit.

One of the first changes I noticed and relished was the setting up of a [US] Marine camp in a field north and west of the station – what is now, in 2004,

3 July 1958 and the 12.25pm Swindon–Didcot 'stopper' arriving at Challow behind No. 6826 'Nannerth Grange'. Fred Strong from Standford-in-the-Vale is going to Steventon Causeway Crossing for his 'late' shift and is walking to fetch his bike. Station master Fred Halford is nearest the camera.

a builders' yard. To most people the word 'marine' conjures up a picture of SAS-type soldiers but these were quite old men. I was interested and thought they were marvellous. Two of them were billeted on us at Petwick Cottage. I thought it was fantastic because they had served in the First World War and they had their rifles with them, and they used to sit in our kitchen and clean their rifles and talk to us about their war experiences.

The camp at Challow station seemed to be a sort of transit depot for shipping materials and spares about the place. As the military side of the station built up, the number of marines increased and a main camp was set up in the Butts Road, Faringdon (very close to the railway station). This became

their barracks but every night and morning some of them came by lorry to Challow station from 8 till 5. A siding was built from the existing sidings at Challow into the marines' depot. We never saw guns but there were lots of lorries. These were left outside the wire so us kids used to go there at night, find some keys and work out how to start the lorries. We even practised driving until our parents found out and then we were in trouble.

During the war local goods train from Swindon all stations to Challow had plenty of work at Shrivenham and often got to Challow late in the afternoon – after Mr Gardiner had gone home. Me and my brother would go to the station with some eggs from our hens and some slices of home-cured

The Up 'Red Dragon', 7.30am Carmarthen–Paddington, passing Challow behind No. 6009 'King Charles II' in September 1960. The 'Kings' made easy work of thirteen coaches through the Vale and was on time through here on a breath of steam. Permanent-way man Arthur Ballard is going to the porters' room to make tea.

A 'Castle' with the 10.45am Paddington–Weston-super-Mare express passing a 'WD'-class 2-8-0 on the Down relief line in 1958.

bacon and we'd get on the engine for a fry-up, sharing the food with the crew who were very glad of something hot and tasty towards the end of a long day. There was so much on the main lines that the goods trip would be held at Challow for very long periods before there was a 'path' back to Swindon.

Station master Gardiner retired in 1944 or 1945. He had given forty-five or fifty years' service to the company but unfortunately his retirement was not noted by the Great Western staff magazine. During the war he had purchased from the company a plot of land immediately north of the goods shed and slightly to the west of his railway carriage chapel, on which he had a contractor build a wooden

bungalow. The end window was opposite the goods shed, several feet above the roadway atop the stone retaining wall holding up the bank.

The next station master was Mr Francis, a very quiet, sombre man. This Mr Francis was probably the promoted ex-district signalling inspector at Swindon. In that role he was a legend: his approach, bowler hat in hand, was viewed with some apprehension by the signalmen. He had an unfortunate attitude towards the work which, as signalman Winter told me, was very much disliked. The latter was, by the account of those who knew him, 'a very rigidly left-wing person, possibly a communist'. He detested Francis and, when the latter came to the signal box to sign the train

Challow passenger/parcels statistics[2]

Year	No. of staff	Annual wage cost £	Total income of station £	Tickets sold	Season tickets	Goods £
1903	9	577	10292	10034	nil	4949
1913	10	736	12160	11691	nil	6006
1923	12	1849	18624	11259	39	8281
1929	12	1974	15395	8266	1	7045
1930	12	2011	15775	7803	3	6665
1933	11	1811	9656	6801	5	5057
1938	11	2048	7288	6566	3	4073

The 6.1pm Didcot–Swindon 'stopper' leaving Challow at about 6.28pm, not long before the station was closed. Seen from the signal box.

register, as he was obliged to do, would ignore his presence completely. He would carry on a conversation with the booking boy – Dennis Brown or Ken Rowlands – and never answer any question from Francis. Francis soon learned to sign the book and leave without a word.[3]

However, Francis followed Gardiner's example and wore his best hat and coat to welcome the arrival of the London passengers for the 7.20 Cheltenham. The last station master at Challow, starting in 1953, was Fred Halford and he continued the tradition of welcoming Challow's clientele, including Sir John Betjeman and his wife Penelope; she drove him in an ancient, wooden-bodied 'station wagon', and the author used to sell her his return ticket to 'Peddington' because he always seemed too absent-minded to buy it for himself.

At the end of the summer timetable in September 1963, the 7.5am Cheltenham – 9.5am Challow – and the 5.5pm Paddington no longer stopped at Challow. Very few people needed to use the local stopping trains, but they continued to run until 5 December 1964. The very last train to call at Challow was the 6.1pm Didcot consisting of two non-corridor coaches hauled by 6112. The driver was A.W. Purnell and the fireman J.W. Sherman, both of Didcot, with a Paddington guard, F.S. Huntingford. The author sent the train away to Uffington after warning the driver of what to expect – a fusillade of exploding fog signals. The author – and some willing helpers – laid them out on the crown of the rail in such a pattern as to sound off 'Half a Pound of Tuppenny Rice' followed by a long 'raspberry'. That used up every fog signal left in the signal box and at the station!

The final Up line page of Challow signal box train register.

CHAPTER 6

Uffington and Faringdon

On 1 June 1864 the brand new Uffington station and the branch line from there to Faringdon opened for business. It stood at 66 miles 45 chains, with the level crossing of the Fernham–Uffington road immediately west of the platform ramps. The branch line was a 3½ miles long, broad gauge, single track with a trailing junction into the GWR Up main line at the 66½ mile post. Uffington station stood at the western end of Baulking cutting, overshadowed on the south by trees and the tall, red-brick 'Junction Hotel' above on the cutting top. From the centre of the village to the station was about 2 miles. The station office building was on the Up platform, which was an 'island' lying north of the Up main with the Faringdon branch alongside the north face of the island. The station building was built in a Brunellian style using red brick with limestone quoins and window casings; a wide canopy extended out on all sides.

None of the Vale stations had a footbridge for passengers to cross the line until fifty or more years after their opening and Steventon never had a footbridge. Uffington had the Fernham road level crossing at the west end of the platforms. Uffington gained a very simple, 'un-Great Western', footbridge in 1897 when the road level crossing was abolished, replaced by an arched, steel, bridge.[1]

The Faringdon branch went out of the station, swinging around from west to north, on the level for about 150yd, before going downhill at 1 in 140 for about 650yd to cross the Ock stream from whence it rose at 1 in 88 for 1½ miles to a summit. After that

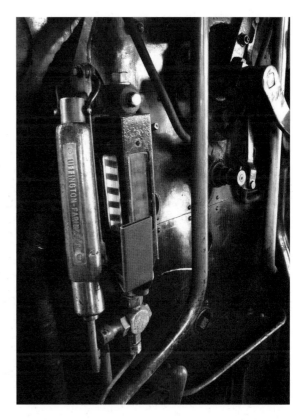

The Uffington–Faringdon train staff.

it fell and rose, and curved this way and that, for 1½ miles into Faringdon station. The engineer of the branch line was a Mr Brodie from Carmarthen and the contractor for building the trackbed was Mr Lewis, a friend of Brodie's also from Carmarthen. The station offices, goods shed and engine shed were built by Malachi Bartlett of Witney.

The broad gauge branch track was not laid in pure Brunellian fashion – with the rails continuously supported by 'longitudinal' sleepers – but with the rails fixed in cast-iron 'chairs' that were spiked to 'cross' sleepers. Thus it was a simple matter to fix one line of chairs at the correct, standard gauge, distance on the sleepers and, over the weekend of 27–28 July 1878, lift one line of rails into the new chairs.

The GWR issued a poster warning that the line would be shut and 'Passengers will not be booked to or from Faringdon during that time but omnibuses or Flys will run between The Crown and The Bull hotels in Faringdon and Uffington Station.' The fare was 1/- 'outside' and 1/6d 'inside'. To catch the 8.30am from Uffington, the traveller had to leave on the 6.30am horse bus. The train journey took ten minutes and in 1878 there were eight trips each way six days a week.

The occupation of the branch line by a train was regulated by a single wooden 'train staff'. It was a piece of varnished oak, 13in long, triangular in cross section, the long edges of the triangle well rounded. A brass plate was let into the surface of the staff, engraved UFFINGTON–FARINGDON. The staff hung in the station untl a signal box was built, when it was kept there. A train was not permitted to leave either station unless the staff was in the possession of the guard, who showed the driver that he had it. In November 1865 the rule was altered so that the staff was handed to the driver, who kept it on the engine but let the guard know he had it.

This was a very safe but inflexible system. The last train from Uffington on Saturday carried the staff to Faringdon and returned with it on the first train on Monday. On Sundays there was no branch train service but there was a need for a morning and evening main line goods train to bring milk and cattle and freight out of Faringdon. The Faringdon porter had to walk the line to Uffington, carrying the staff, so that the engine and the brake van from a main line goods could go down the branch – taking the porter to Faringdon – to pick up the outward-bound wagons and haul them back to the main line train, the latter being stored on a siding at

Looking east off the Fernham Road bridge in 1963. *R.C. RILEY/TRAINSPORT TREASURY*

Looking east from the Down main line, c. 1958. R.M. CASSERLEY

Uffington. The staff was then at Uffington for the evening engine and van to go to Faringdon and back. The Uffington porter then had to walk it back to Faringdon for the first train out on Monday – and then walk home to the village.

This mad system was tolerated until June 1882 when a 'ticket' was introduced as a supplementary staff. A metal key was fitted to the end of the staff to unlock the ticket box. With the ticket box lid unlocked, a ticket could be taken out but the staff was locked into the box until the lid was closed and locked. The last passenger train to Faringdon on Saturday went down with an authorizing ticket and the staff remained at Uffington for the Sunday morning goods. The Sunday evening engine and van from the main line took the staff to Faringdon and came back – with the milk vans – on a ticket, issued by the station master, leaving the staff for the first train on Monday morning.

With the introduction of the ticket, any number of trains could follow the first, each with a ticket, so that a signal box, 7 × 5ft, had to be built at Faringdon to accommodate interlocked signal and point levers and an electric block telegraph instrument working to Uffington signal box. This was because the dispatching signalman had to know that the line was clear through to the other end of the line before he let a second train depart.

The branch engine and its crew were stationed at Faringdon, where coal and water supplies were kept – there was no locomotive water supply at Uffington until 1897. There was no turntable at either end of the line and the company had given a written promise to the Board of Trade that only tank engines would work the line. Records exist for the locomotive department at Faringdon covering 1902–33 and these show that forty-nine different tank engines were stationed there in thirty years. The majority of them were the 0–4–2 14xx engines, but there were 0–6–0 saddle tanks and also for six months an 0–6–0 goods tender engine, in contravention of the undertaking.

The branch grew busier as industry developed around the station at Faringdon and in the town. In 1896, the year in which the Uffington station layout was enlarged, there were eleven round trips on the branch and, wartime excepted, that lasted until 1933 when the engine shed was closed and the branch engine and coaches came up each day from Swindon.

On 18 September 1909 the Army held a large-scale 'war game' over an area bounded by the

The station from the Down platform. The Faringdon branch curving north. R.M. CASSERLEY

Cotswolds to the north, the Berkshire Downs to the South, Swindon to the west and Oxford to the east. Dozens of regiments took part, including all the Guards regiments. Faringdon town became the centre of operations for two weeks and the Faringdon and Fairford branch lines were to carry all the troop train movements into and out of the area and during the 'war'. The train staff and ticket system was – for the two weeks – replaced by the electric train token system, an instrument in Uffington and Faringdon signal boxes. Although it has always been officially denied, Crown Prince Wilhelm of Germany (1882–1951) the son of Kaiser Wilhelm II, was present in Faringdon throughout the manoeuvres and maybe travelled on the Faringdon branch train.[2]

The greatest service of trains on the branch was 1912 to 1914 with sixteen round trips a day, taking seven minutes each way. In 1912 two engines worked the line: one on the line, and one away on some other line or having works attention. These were 1436 and 1443, both '517'-class 0-4-2 tanks. These were of a class introduced by George Armstrong at the Wolverhampton works in 1868. They were so well designed that they became a numerous class, and some were still at work in 1932 when a modernized version of them was introduced – the '1400'-class 0-4-2 tanks that were still in use in 1964. The full accountancy calculated cost of working the branch line in 1912 was £1,750 8s 6d.

In 1912 the branch passenger train consisted of a four-wheeled third-class carriage (No. 327), a four-wheeled first- and third-class carriage (No. 7881), and a four-wheeled passenger brake van. Besides that there were two milk churn-carrying vans and a freight train guard's van. Dozens of goods wagons worked over the line, both general freight open wagons and box vans; on market days twenty or more empty cattle wagons were brought onto the branch. Other rolling stock recorded as being used included 'Python', flat-bed carriage trucks, 'Serpent' furniture vans and 'Mica' vans for carrying meat for human consumption. Until the 1920s and the rise of the infernal combustion engine, the branch grew busier as the standard of living rose and more of everything was consumed.

The single needle telegraph preceded the use of telephones on the railway by many decades and even in 1940 there were many places – Oxford station was one – where the telegraph was more widely used than the telephone for long-distance communication. The electro-magnetic deflection of the needle from vertical to left or right, repeated in a coded sequence, spelled out a letter. To reduce the time it took to send a telegraph message, the mid-19th century railway invented 'texting': the use of a single word to convey a message. Hence 'Serpent' or 'Mica'; other words meant several sentences. A code book was issued.

The branch worked hard to supply the people of Faringdon. In 1912 Great Western accountants made a detailed study of the cost of everything happening on the branch and concluded that, in 1912, it cost £1,757 8s 6d to run.[3] The income of Faringdon station in 1913 – there is no record of 1912 – was £17,667.[4] Main line excursion trains were advertised in Faringdon and the main line train would stop at Uffington to pick up and set down the Faringdon trippers. Faringdon people could have a reasonable time on the beach at Weston-super-Mare, or in Savernake Forest, or at Cheltenham or Newbury races, or visit Windsor Castle or London.

After the First World War, buses and cars began to make their presence felt. In 1923 the train service was eleven round trips each day and the company began to ask questions about its profitability. The goods traffic kept up its importance for longer, but passenger traffic was wide open to competition even from the slow, bone-shaking buses on the roads of the period.

In March 1926, the assistant superintendent of the line, H.L. Wilkinson, was commissioned to visit thirty-six short, single-track GWR branch lines to study their utility. His terms of reference included such questions as 'How far would the abolition of locomotive power reduce costs?' – i.e. by using a steam rail motor – and 'Is there a case for lifting the rails and laying a road for the company's motor buses?'[5]

He was brutally honest about the Faringdon branch: it had had its day.

The working of the Faringdon branch, with passengers having to change, gives an advantage in time and convenience to road transport and private cars are easier. The remoteness of the junction station is also a disadvantage, which was not the case when the line was built and time and convenience were not of paramount importance. The general and perishable traffic needing quick transit is subject to road competition and is conveyed by mixed train if the traffic is regular. [The goods wagon containing the traffic was attached to the rear of a branch passenger train.] Time is lost attaching such traffic and siding accommodation is often insufficient for wagons to be stabled pending collection by the branch or main line train. This lack is in some part due to heavy goods such as coal or grain occupying sidings as it waits to be unloaded or to be collected by a special trip.

A steam locomotive on the branch costs 1/6 3/4d per mile, an auto train 1/5d [that is, a locomotive pushing a carriage where the engine can be driven from a driver's compartment at the front of the coach] and a steam rail motor car 1/4d per mile. A road motor bus could operate for 1/03/4d – but only a steam locomotive can haul freight.

Steam rail motors are unsuited to branch line work owing to the steep gradients encountered and their inability to haul freight. These were first used on the Eastern Counties Railway in 1849 and the fact that there are now only ninety-one at work in the country – and this company owns fifty-three – demonstrates their unsuitability for general railway work.

The system of signalling using the train staff and ticket, assisted by block telegraph, is cheap and effective, saving the cost of two token instruments. Whilst I feel that branch line engine sheds should be closed wherever possible I do not think that this should be done at Faringdon as the miles of 'light' running to and from Swindon would be wasteful. To save the cost of electricity at present bought from the Eagle electric light company of Faringdon, might it not be possible for the branch engine to supply steam to a turbine-driven dynamo while supplying steam to the well pump and thus charge batteries which could be used to illuminate the station offices at Faringdon?

Faringdon passenger/parcels statistics[6]

Year	No. of staff	Annual wage cost £	Total income of station £	Tickets sold	Season tickets	Goods £
1903	7	515	15678	18056	nil	8414
1913	9	741	17667	19023	nil	10208
1923	11	1783	27537	14051	5	17529
1929	10	1717	21704	9281	14	12639
1930	11	1760	21690	8168	18	14047
1933	8	1457	11036	4569	6	8807
1938	8	1273	19829	1445	2	8627

Mr C.B. Collett, Chief Mechanical Engineer of the GWR, was consulted and he rejected the idea. Wilkinson's report showed that goods traffic over the line consisted of the same items in 1925 as in 1875: milk, cattle, hay, roadstone, coal, round timber and planks, and one addition – tin plate boxes.

The directors' decision was: 'Very little can be done to improve the situation at Faringdon but we will keep an eye on the situation.'

Income at Faringdon was affected by the General Strike of 1926, but in 1927 it rose to a peak of £23,800, equal to 1923. Thereafter it fell annually until in 1933 it was only £11,000. But there must have been

The west end of the station, peaceful and sunny amid the parkland scenery of the White Horse Vale, c. 1957. What a joy it was to work here in steam days! PENDON MUSEUM

some very loyal core users because, in spite of fare and freight rate increases, Faringdon station still took in £21,000 during 1938. At Uffington in that year the station took £1,772 – £500 more than the wage bill. But the company still did not abandon the branch. In July 1928 the Sunday morning milk train out of Faringdon was reinstated and the passenger service continued at eleven trains each way per day. In that year a road motor was based at Faringdon for rural collection and delivery – 'country lorry' – services. This was the first such service to be introduced on the Great Western.

The last day of the branch passenger train service was 29 December 1951. During the day many people bought a ticket for a ride on the branch, people who had never used it before. A crowd larger than any previously seen there – regiments of soldiers excepted – gathered at Faringdon to see the last train, the 8.35pm, leave. Faringdon's station master, J.V. Hale was in attendance, as were Arthur Westcott, station master at Uffington, and E.W. Major, assistant station master at Swindon. Also up from Swindon were Mr and Mrs Coles who formed a two-piece band on the platform and played 'Auld Lang Syne', which the crowd sang with gusto. The throng crammed themselves into the two carriages and Arthur Westcott's daughter got on the engine and tugged the whistle chain for the seven-minute ride to Uffington to encourage the musicians and crowd to play and sing louder. Bedlam reigned all the way to Uffington and on the platform at Uffington as 'Auld Lang Syne' was sung over and over again. Exhausted, the crowd dispersed, some to cars waiting for them, many to the Junction Hotel.

The passenger service had lasted 87½ years and forty quarterly season ticket holders at Faringdon now had to find other ways of getting to their daily work or college.

Main line passenger train service for Uffington in 1964

Down Uffington

7.50am Didcot	Swindon	8.24 – 25am
1.58pm Didcot	Swindon	2.27 – 28am
6.01pm Didcot	Swindon	6.33 – 34pm

Up

6.45am Swindon	Didcot	7.05 – 06am
4.15pm Swindon	Didcot	4.28 – 29pm
5.51pm Swindon	Didcot	6.12 – 13pm

At the end of 1952 Uffington station's passenger income was £1,000; it remained at around that level until 1959, but its goods traffic had vanished. In 1955 the Faringdon railway lorry called at the station to collect any parcels.

Faringdon's freight traffic continued to be brought to Uffington. The 7am Didcot–Uffington 'Fly', calling at all stations, ran on Mondays, Wednesdays and Fridays and the 8.10am Swindon–Faringdon, calling at Shrivenham, ran daily. The author worked Uffington box for a year 1961–62 and on the days when the Didcot 'Fly' ran, the station came to life with the sound of two engines shunting: whistles, the bark of the engines and the jostling of the buffers as the two trains sorted out the exchange wagons.

The branch closed to freight traffic on 1 July 1963 and during 1964 the track was lifted. The armless tubular steel post of the branch Up distant signal remained like a grave marker for many years afterwards.

The station closed for ever on 5 December 1964.

CHAPTER 7

Shrivenham

Shrivenham station stood at the 71 mile 45 chain point from Paddington and was a bare ¾ mile from the village. It was the only classic Brunel station of the original three. It had knapped flint walls, Bath stone quoins and window casings. The office and waiting room windows were mullioned, the office had a bay window with sloping Bath stone cills and there were blind 'arrow slits'. The roof, which was

Shrivenham station from the Ashbury road bridge, looking west, c. 1900. The station buildings are Brunellian, 1840. The signal box is an original GWR 1874 design. The Up line signal posts are very tall. At the foot of the nearest post are two lamps on a hoisting cable: one for the starting signal, one for Ashbury crossing's distant signal. PENDON MUSEUM

Looking east on the Up platform under the 1840 canopy, c. 1958.
PENDON MUSEUM

almost flat, extended on all four sides to form a wide awning, which was level, and all of this covered entirely with what appeared to be lead. This was perhaps the most handsome of the four designs Brunel drew up for wayside stations.

Lord Barrington of Beckett Park, Shrivenham, was the main landowner and since early 1840 had been a director of the Great Western, sitting on the London committee of management. Brunel had just a little prejudice against 'titles' and in Lord Barrington's case he had an extra grudge in that Barrington had prevented him from making his route west of Steventon to Wootton Bassett absolutely perfect. So no special favours, just one of Brunel's standard designs.

The station was opened on 17 December 1840.

Shrivenham station in those early days was a carefree sort of place, rather like the rest of the Great Western. Everything was yet to be learned. Misdemeanours were commonplace and each and every occasion required a trip to Paddington to stand in before the board of directors to answer the charge and to either admit the offence – which many did – or to defend oneself if one thought there was a chance of retaining the job.

On 21 July 1842, Mr Quarrington, the night policeman at Shrivenham, was summoned to Paddington to be 'examined upon the subject of the theft of a bale of bacon while he was on duty, in charge of the station during the night'. Quarrington was able to convince the directors that it was not he who had stolen it, but had to plead guilty to the charge of not being aware of the theft. He was fined 10/-, half a crown a week to be deducted from his wages.[1]

The awful crash at Shrivenham on 10 May 1848, leaving five dead and thirteen injured, was an unprecedented event on the Great Western until the Norton Fitzwarren crash of November 1890 – which happened in spite of a relatively modern signalling system. The derailment at Shipton-on-Cherwell on Christmas Eve 1874, when thirty-four died and sixty-five were injured, was due to a defective wheel rather than a collision.

At about 3.10pm that 10 May, porter Weybury started to walk from the station west, into the sidings to move a van of merchandise into the goods shed for unloading. There were two wagons standing in front of it, a horse box and a cattle truck. There was room for all three to stand alongside the loading platform in the shed, but instead Weybury chose to turn the points at the western end of the goods shed for the Up main and then, with the assistance of 'porter' Willoughby, to roll the two wagons onto the Up main to get the van past them into the shed.

Looking east off the station footbridge at some time between 1935 and 1939. An Up train has just passed, a Down goods train is in the loop. PENDON MUSEUM

The wagons could be set moving by the use of a 'pinch bar' – an 8ft-long ash pole with a curved iron-shod end. The curved end would be thrust between the rail and the wheel, the long handle pushed down with small effort and the wagon would start to roll. Many times as a 'lad porter' – which in 1960 was still a formal title – the author used the pinch bar in Challow's 1840 vintage goods shed; the pinch bar looked as if it might have been as old as the building.

Weybury did not ask permission from Pargetter, the station policeman, to occupy the Up main. Pargetter was expecting the 12 noon Exeter express and was standing by the level crossing of the main road from Shrivenham to Ashbury at the east end of the station platforms. The noon Exeter was scheduled to leave Swindon at 2.53pm and so it should pass Shrivenham about 3.08pm – the Exeter expresses were the fastest trains in the world at that time. The driver on this day was Robert Roscoe, a 'top link' Paddington man. The train consisted of a mail van, three second- and three first-class carriages. Together with about 150 passengers and the content of the mail van, the engine was hauling around 65 tons. Roscoe's engine was 'Sultan', a Gooch express engine with 8ft diameter driving wheels. The train left Swindon twenty-one minutes late at 3.16pm. The GWR Regulation at that time was that drivers were not to make up any time, so Roscoe would have to come through Shrivenham at around 50mph.

At 3.20pm Weybury and Willoughby had pushed the wagons half in, half out of the siding, leaving the leading horse box on the Up main and the cattle truck just foul, and had gone back to roll the merchandise van into the goods shed. Pargetter,

A 'Castle' – one of the 'Earl of' series – passing through Shrivenham about 1958. The Victoria Hotel is across the way. PENDON MUSEUM

standing at the opposite end of the station, said he did not know what the porters were doing but he would have seen what was happening had he kept a good lookout to the west – from which direction the overdue express would come.

At 3.26 'Sultan' came roaring into Shrivenham station. It first caught the cattle truck a glancing blow and then hit the horse box almost end-on. Both vehicles disintegrated. One pair of horse box wheels, the axle bent double, flew through the air and wedged in the office doorway of the station, hitting the station master, Corbett Hudson as he ran to he doorway from his office. He was hurt but not killed. The horse box roof came off in one piece, sliced off 'Sultan's chimney and flew on, Roscoe and his fireman ducking just in time. The flying debris of splintered wood smashed coaches and knocked five passengers onto the track, killing them.

'Porter' Willoughby was not a GWR employee but was doing the work of the real porter – Copley – who was away from the station pleading illness, but in fact had found himself another job and had rented his job to Willoughby and was drinking the rent money Willoughby was paying. Porter Weybury and Constable Pargetter were arrested and put on trial for manslaughter, and both were found guilty at Berkshire Assizes. They were imprisoned and dismissed from their jobs at Shrivenham.[2]

One and a quarter miles west of Shrivenham, the 'Acorn Bridge' is a fine twin-arch bridge that carries the railway over the derelict Wilts & Berks Canal and the Swindon–Oxford road. The work was contracted to the very second-rate William Ranger.[3] Ranger employed skilful craftsmen but he was a very poor manager and always short of money and equipment. Here is a letter Brunel had to write to him on 3 June 1837 concerning the Acorn Bridge:

It was with great astonishment and regret that I observed when last at the Acorn Bridge that nothing was being done towards the long delayed erection of the steam engine. I cannot for one moment suppose that anybody would pretend to get the excavation for this bridge without some means of pumping and I see no preparations for any other means than that of an engine and there appears as regards this some cause of delay which is not communicated to me and unless I have immediately a clear and satisfactory explanation of all the present circumstances of your future plans and unless I can be satisfied that these plans are not only efficient but will immediately be carried into execution I shall wait no longer but without delay take all those steps which I consider necessary to regain a portion of the time which has been negligently wasted and proceed with the work in such a manner as I may find necessary. I regret being driven to this decision but the monumental dilatoriness of your proceedings and latterly by the apparent abandonment of all attempts to proceed leaves me no alternative. I shall feel obliged by an immediate reply.

Employing second-rate contractors retarded the construction of the railway, caused Brunel a lot of extra work and the company extra expenditure in legal fees, and delayed the opening of the railway.

In 1863 Shrivenham station was quite heavily staffed, and indeed this seemed to be the case at least up to 1938. Until 1874 there were five policemen stationed here to attend to the disc and crossbar signalling, the level crossing at the east end of the platforms and the Ashbury lane half a mile further east:

- Station master   1 at £90 per annum
- Policemen   3 at 17/- per week
                    1 at 16/- per week
                    1 at 15/- per week
- Porters   2 at 17/- per week
                    1 at 15/- per week
- Office porter   1 at 16/- per week

The station was closed for all purposes from 5 December 1964.

Shrivenham passenger/parcels statistics[4]

Year	No. of staff	Annual wage cost £	Total income of station £	Tickers sold	Season tickets	Goods £
1903	17	1107	9987	16302	nil	3499
1913	18	1207	9970	17345	nil	3549
1923	18	2971	16723	14547	43	7764
1929	20	3372	12051	8878	32	5803
1930	19	3407	10333	9667	31	3837
1933	18	2975	5186	7287	52	7440
1938	20	4783	7798	9010	67	6564

CHAPTER 8

Stratton Park Halt and the Highworth Branch

Stratton Park Halt

The halt was opened in November 1933.[1] It consisted of a wooden platform on each side of the line, in a cutting, at 75 miles 5 chains. The village of Stratton St Margeret was ¾ mile north along the main road. Passengers reached it down footpaths from the bridge carrying the A419 Marlborough–Cirencester road over the line. The GWR kindly provided, for the comfort of their passengers, a corrugated iron hut on each platform, the sort of hut normally used for storing paraffin.

In 1936 the halt was served by all of the 'all stations' passenger trains, Up and Down: eight Down, seven Up. On the Down line the first was 7.24am Shrivenham which had the unusual destination of Andover Junction; this called at 7.31am.[2] The others were:

No. 7019 'Fowey Castle' with the 10.35 Kensington tanks in the cutting west of Marston West, c. 1962. The latter's Down starting signal is at the right of the picture, heading towards Stratton Park halt. MIKE ESAU

Down

- 6.52am Reading – Swindon 8.31am
- 8.11am Slough – Gloucester 10.36am
- 9.20am Slough – Swindon 11.32am
- 12.33pm Didcot – Swindon 1.26pm
- 2.38pm Reading – Swindon 4.14pm
- 2.30pm Paddington – Swindon 6.40pm
- 8.20pm Didcot – Swindon 9.6pm

Up

- 6.55am Swindon – Paddington 6.59am
- 7.48am Swindon – Didcot 7.52am
- 10.22am Swindon – Didcot 10.26am
- 12 noon Swindon – Didcot 12.4pm
- 2.00pm Swindon – Paddington 2.4pm
- 4.30pm Swindon – Faringdon 4.34pm
- 2.10pm Swansea – Paddington 7.39pm

In 1934, 1,727 tickets were sold, bringing in £64 8s 89d per ticket. In 1935, 450 tickets for £11 5s 8d per ticket.[3] From 1936 the accounts for the halt were subsumed into Swindon Junction's account. There were still six trains every weekday calling in each direction in 1960 but with even less result. In spite of the spectacular lack of interest shown in the halt it remained open until the end of local train service on 5 December 1964. It was probably more valued by young lads as a platform for watching the magnificent spectacle of the trains passing, from the long, lumbering coal trains, to the sharp crackling 'fully fitted' vacuum goods, the heavy milk tanker trains and the ordinary expresses. Most of all, it was a wonderful place to get the best thrill from the 'Cheltenham Flyer' or 'Bristolian' skimming the boards and shivering the timbers of the poor old place.

Looking east at the halt, c. 1960; Highworth Junction's Down distant signal is on the right. GREAT WESTERN TRUST

Stratton station, looking south on 31 March 1962. DON LOVELOCK

The Highworth Branch

The Swindon & Highworth Railway Company obtained its Act of Parliament on 29 July 1875.[4] The Board of Trade inspection in March 1881 revealed serious errors in its construction, leading to a refusal to sanction its use. The company had no money to improve matters and so, very remarkably, the GWR agreed to buy it and amalgamation took place on 10 August 1882. The great company brought the line up to the normal standard of construction and safety and the Board of Trade sanctioned its opening, which took place on 9 May 1883.

The branch line left the GWR main line at Highworth Junction and, notwithstanding the GWR's attention, trains still ran over a cheaply constructed single track, with less than standard-clearance overbridges, extreme gradients and serpentine curves to reach Highworth station, 5 miles 48 chains further on. The clearances through the bridges on the branch were less than elsewhere on the GWR, and a 'Highworth' loading gauge was installed at Swindon goods yard under which branch goods train vehicles had to pass so as to be sure they would pass clear under the bridges.

The GWR 1929 Working Time Table shows that coaches on the branch were all four-wheeled vehicles. Because the track was so lightly constructed only the lightest tank engines of the GWR were permitted to run on the line – these were the 0–4–2 tanks of the '517' class and their later replacements, the 1932 built '48xx' class 0–4–2 tanks. In emergencies the lightest possible 0–6–0 tank engines were permitted, but on no account were tender engines to be used on the line.[5]

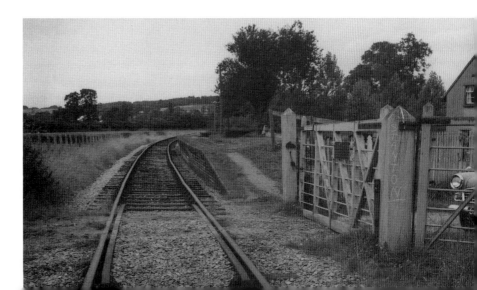

Stanton station – or halt, c. 1962.
GREAT WESTERN TRUST

Highworth station from the south, 31 March 1962. DON LOVELOCK

No. 1658 at the south end of Highworth station on a 1 in 44 gradient on 31 March 1962. The engine brought the train in, 'hooked off and ran round', then ran forward to get onto the south end of the coaches. DON LOVELOCK

A wooden train staff was used to ensure that only one train at a time occupied the single track between the junction and Highworth. The first station was Stratton, 1 mile 24 chains from Highworth Junction. The next was Stanton, at 3 miles 18 chains, after which the line passed over the Cricklade Road crossing to the next station, Hannington, at 4 miles 32 chains. The terminus, Highworth station, 5 miles 48 chains from the Junction, was at the end of a gradient rising from Hannington at 1 in 86 and 1 in 44.

There was no engine shed at Highworth so the daily train service always started from Swindon. The maximum speed on the line was 25mph, subject to six lower limits including a maximum of 15mph dropping down from Highworth to Hannington. In 1910 the 4.35am Swindon (empty coaches) worked back as the 5.15am Highworth–Swindon passenger train. There were six more passenger trains after that, with two additional services on a Saturday. It is very likely that one of these trains also conveyed empty and loaded milk churns in the specially built milk vans.

Highworth station building, c. 1960.

On Sundays the 7am Swindon–Highworth passenger returning from Highworth at 7.45am and the 6.5pm Swindon, coming back at 7pm from Highworth, would have taken out milk and brought back empty churns. The 1929 timetable orders that the 7.20am (Sundays) Highworth–Swindon service was to be marshalled in this order: engine; milk vans for Southall, Clapham Junction, South Lambeth and Paddington; and a brake third-class passenger coach. From the end of the summer timetable in 1933, the service was reduced to four passenger trains per day, seven on Saturdays and a daily goods train.

The needs of the First World War created industrialization in the fields beside the branch. A rail-connected factory making explosive and filling shells with explosive was built in the district of Gorse Hill, about 400yd north of Highworth Junction, to the west of the branch line. A 12 × 10ft wooden signal box called 'Stratton Factory', with ten levers, was brought into use to work the junction on 18 February 1917. Electric train token (ETT) instruments were installed there and at Highworth Junction. The signal box was closed and ETT working abolished on 28 July 1919, and the wooden train staff was reinstated.[6]

Looking south from Highworth station, c. 1960.

In 1940 the Vickers Supermarine aircraft factory at Southampton, which built Spitfires, was heavily bombed, and a replacement factory was built by Vickers-Armstrongs in the fields north-east of the village of South Marston, south-east of Stanton Fitzwarren. This was rail-connected to the Highworth branch with the junction signal box, 2 miles 10 chains from Highworth Junction called Kingsdown Road, and opened for traffic on 17 February 1942.[7] The ETT system of train control operated to Highworth Junction and the wooden train staff from Kingsdown Road to Highworth. The 'Vickers Branch' was a single track siding about a mile long into the factory. The war also brought to the lower end of the branch the Plessey company, producing electric equipment for the war effort.

The public passenger service to Highworth was withdrawn from 2 March 1953, but there was sufficient goods traffic as far as Kingsdown Road to retain the ETT system. When Kingsdown Road box switched out the signalman released a token in Highworth Junction box. The morning and evening free trains for Swindon railway factory workmen continued to run until 3 August 1962, and the daily goods train continued to run through to Highworth until 6 August. Kingsdown Road box was taken out of use on that day.[8]

Combined Highworth Branch passenger/parcels statistics[9]

Year	No. of staff	Annual wage cost £	Total income of station £	Tickets sold	Season tickets	Goods £
1903	10	551	13274	70792	nil	6169
1913	10	625	13794	53614	nil	9128
1923	12	2148	22706	40524	801	11221
1929	12	1868	20334	24489	723	11103
1930	12	1757	18961	19624	696	9922
1933	10	1372	12530	773	524	9233
1938	9	1251	6620	8400	390	4903

CHAPTER 9

Hay Lane and Swindon Junction

On 6 October 1840 the directors 'Resolved: that the principal Locomotive Station and Repairing Shops be established at or near the junction with the Cheltenham and Great Western Union Railway at Swindon'.[1] This was accepting Daniel Gooch's recommendation to the directors, that: 'A large station at Swindon would enable us to keep all our bank engines for the Wootton Bassett incline at Swindon instead of having a separate station for that purpose at the bottom of the Incline and at any rate it would be necessary to have a considerable station at Swindon to work the Cheltenham line.' Gooch recommended a locomotive station, not a passenger station.

In this same minute of October 1840 the directors resolved that 'the Principal Passenger Station be fixed for Swindon near to the Engine Station at Wootton Bassett on the road leading to Marlborough and Chippenham near the approach to the town.'[2] This place was Hay Lane at the 80¼ mile post from Paddington.

Hay Lane, marooned inside miles of quagmire roads, was to be called in the timetable 'Wootton Bassett Road'. In the company minutes, by Brunel and by the inspecting officer for the board of trade it was referred to as 'Hay Lane'.

The first mention in GWR minutes of a passenger station at the site of the existing Swindon station was made by the C&GWU, responding to Brunel.

At a Board meeting of the GWR directors on 3 November 1840, an extract from the minutes of the C&GWU was read out. The C&GWU stated that:

> Mr Brunel having explained an arrangement for a joint depot at Swindon for this company and the Great Western Company which appears to be of mutual benefit to both companies. To the effect that the Great Western Company would require the land purchased by this (C&GWU) Company from Mr Sheppard for the Engine Station for both companies. Resolved: That this [C&GWU] company agrees to make over to the Great Western Company such land, when the same may be required, provided the arrangement be so made as that all requisite accommodation, both at the Engine House and Passenger Station, for working the Cheltenham line separately, is reserved to this Company, together with proper roads and access thereto from the canal and adjoining High Roads.

Having discussed this suggestion, the Great Western directors resolved that:

> It is expedient to admit and confirm the principles upon which the Cheltenham & Great Western Union company offer to part with the land at Swindon, it being understood that an equitable allowance of cost of any buildings, roads or works

required for the separate use of the Cheltenham company – or for their use jointly with the Great Western company is to be borne by them whenever they may claim the advantage of such appropriation, after the expiration of the lease and upon resuming possession of their Line to be separately worked by that Company.[3]

The leasing was found to be an unsatisfactory way to run a railway because the lessor company was still a power in its own right, and the lessee was a tenant, not an entirely free agent. On 10 May 1844 the C&GWU amalgamated with the GWR.

The railway from Bristol to Bath was opened on 31 August 1840. From Faringdon Road to Hay Lane was opened on 17 December 1840. This is very strange since there were no facilities for passengers at that place at that time and in any case road access to Hay Lane was all but impossible at that time of year. Passenger and goods traffic from Bath and Bristol, Gloucester, Cheltenham and Cirencester continued to use the Faringdon Road station: 'the roads to Cirencester are almost impassable from Hay Lane and from the same cause the Bristol and Bath road traffic also continued to use Faringdon Road'.[4]

J.H. Gandell applied for the contract to build Hay Lane station and on 3 November 1840 the directors resolved 'that the said offer should be accepted and the Engineer instructed to give the requisite Plans to Mr Gandell for the immediate erection of the buildings at Hay Lane'.[5]

On 9 November Gandell sub-contracted the work to John Streat of Shrivenham.[6]

The Inspecting Officer for the Board of Trade, General Sir Frederick Smith came, in November 1840 to inspect the station. Station construction had not begun, but the construction of the engine repair shop and maintenance depot were well advanced under the contractor S&J Rigby. In his report Sir Frederick mistook this for work on the permanent station: 'Although Hay Lane station is merely intended as a temporary terminus the company are forming it as regards sidings, switches and other mechanical arrangements in the same extensive

and substantial manner as is their ordinary practise at permanent terminals.'

On 26 November 1840 Brunel wrote to Gandell:

I am sorry to see that no progress whatever is made, no directions even given and on the contrary our work is proceeding without any preparations for the refreshment rooms at Hay Lane. The cottages also are very backward. I understood that they were all in frame somewhere – I should feel much relieved to know where.

It is only fair that I should give you notice that I consider it my duty to do what I can to prevent you ever having another opportunity of disappointing us so grossly as you have in every case as yet – and that I shall now immediately urge upon the directors the necessity of making arrangements with somebody else for building the requisite refreshment rooms at Hay Lane.[7]

John Streat's men had started work around 10 November but Gandell declared himself insolvent on the 23rd and Streat ceased work. GWR 'requested and ordered him' to continue the works but denied their liability to pay John Streat for any of the works, their case being that he was not the man with whom they had contracted to build the place.

The company then offered to pay Streat for the work he did subsequent to 23 December but Streat refused this until they agreed to pay him from the start. The case was put before an arbitrator, Thomas Donaldson. Donaldson ruled that

since 23 December 1840 bricklayers, carpenters, plumbers, masons and others have been working in and about the completion of thirteen cottage and the erection of five dormitory cottages and also certain stables and a coach house and I award, order and determine that the value of the works performed by John Streat are of the value of £1,767 5 shillings and three pence.[8]

The land and all the buildings thereon were Gandell's property – rented to the company. But as Gandell was insolvent one would suppose that they

The classical style of Swindon station, 1961.

were now in the hands of his liquidators. However, a minute of the directors' meeting on 5 January 1841 records that:

> Mr Gandell proposed that he should receive £500 in lieu of the Fee [sic] of the land on which he is to erect his buildings at Hay Lane, undertaking either to repay the £500 to the company when the station is abandoned, or, to leave the Cottages and Sleeping Room to become the company's property either for removal or for permanent occupation – and in case the station becomes permanent or is not removed within twelve months of the opening of Hay Lane, either to repay the £500 at that time or to give up the property of the cottages.[9]

Gandell's proposal was accepted by the directors. It was at this January 1841 meeting that the directors resolved that:

> The Engineer and General Superintendent of the Line be required to consider with as little delay as possible and report the best mode of forming the junctions between the Cheltenham & Great Western Union Railway with the line at Swindon as well as to submit a plan of the necessary buildings there.

On 31 May 1841 the Great Western route from Hay Lane to Chippenham was opened as well as the leased C&GWU route from Swindon to Cirencester. Swindon station was incomplete but there was enough of it there for it to be opened to passengers on that day. Swindon station refreshment rooms were not ready for use until 14 July 1842. The Great Western Railway's main line from Paddington to Bristol Temple Meads was then complete, although the authorized branch line from Thingley to Trowbridge and Bradford-on-Avon had not been started.

Hay Lane–'Wootton Bassett Road' remained in use until Wootton Bassett station opened in August 1842.

Swindon station consisted of two 'island' platforms. Each island platform carried a two-storey main block. The ground floor design was produced in Brunel's office in Duke Street, Westminster and the first floor was designed in the offices of Francis Thompson, the architect of the North Midland Railway. The station as an operational whole is a replica of Normanton station, designed by Brunel's friend, Robert Stephenson, in 1840, for North Midland Railway.

The two-storey buildings were 170ft long by 37ft wide and were built of Swindon stone, rendered in

Swindon station from the road in 1965. The building was probably erected in 1872–3. The GWR designed the new building in harmony with the original building, but a later extension clashes. The booking office was at street level, administrative offices above.

cement to cover natural discolorations and imperfections in the stone.[10] The two blocks had a stately dignity. This was achieved using a mildly classical style. The east and west ends of the surviving block retain its 1842 Grecian pediment. The verticals of the full height extension, standing slightly proud of the gable end, with its upper storey, square mullioned, window, under a plain cornice, adds to the impression. All along the length of the eaves of the building the simple cornice continues with the classical windows in a row beneath.

The two blocks were identical in external plan except that the block on the northern platform had its first-class passengers' accommodation at the west end and the southern block had the first-class rooms at the east end. The staff sleeping and eating quarters and kitchens were in the basements. The ground floors were divided between the first- and second-class ticket holders[11] with separate entrances of course. The central space between the two classes contained the stairs leading up to the enclosed footbridge. The footbridge was also accessible from stairs rising from the platforms. By this all passengers crossed the lines or gained access to the 'Queen's Hotel'. The northern block held the first- and second-class bedrooms, the southern

block the day rooms and coffee rooms. Originally there was no subway. A new booking office was built in 1872–3 and perhaps it was at this stage that a subway was excavated.

On 2 February 1841 The plans for the Swindon station and its passenger accommodation were laid before the Board.[12] Brunel had been wildly optimistic in his original estimate of £2.5 million for the construction of the line from Bristol to London. By the end of 1841, £6,282,000 had been spent, more than half of that was a debt, not capital raised from sale of shares.[13] The company had a huge mortgage debt and was unable to pay cash to S&J Rigby to build the locomotive repair shops, the station and the railway village. Economies had to be found. The minute of 2 February 1841 read:

> The refreshment rooms, waiting rooms, water closets and every other accommodation in the buildings required for passengers at Swindon, together with sheds over the lines, covered platforms on each side and the rooms required for cooking and also for lodging persons employed in the refreshment rooms are to be provided by the Contractor in consideration of the profits to be derived from that business.

The north side of Exeter Street, looking towards the 'Glue Pot' pub in 1974. The cottages are tiny. The windows on each side of the front door belong to separate dwellings. Brunel designed for public show as much as for living in.

A building lease is to be granted to the Contractor … for 99 years subject to be terminated by breach of contract.

The Contractor to undertake that the business shall be carried on in a manner and upon a principle quite equal in every respect to the best refreshment plan of any other railway and to the approbation of the Chairman and Deputy Chairman of the company. The prices or charges to be regulated by a tariff to be approved by the same.

Other usual covenants are to be introduced especially for the quiet and proper occupation of the buildings so as not to interfere in manner with the rights and duties of the company and their servants.

All persons employed by the contractor are to be subject to the control of the company and to be dismissed on the demand of the directors.

Cottages not exceeding 300 are to be built by the contractor and the cost of the station and the cottages is not to exceed £50,000 the number of cottages to be reduced if the cost should exceed that amount. The company will take the cottages on a 30-year lease at a rent not exceeding 6% of the cost of building.

This Minute was amended in October when the 300 cottages were not to cost more than £35,000

to build.[14] Messers Rigby were informed that the directors will give them the contract on the terms specified.[15]

This minute made no mention of stopping passenger trains for ten minutes at Swindon but this obligation was included in the lease contract of the refreshment rooms and hotel by the Great Western to Messrs Rigby which was signed on 13 December 1841. The Great Western was clearly seriously embarrassed, financially, to have signed such a document in order to get their staff cottages, station and repair works built – and having put themselves at the mercy of the Rigby brothers they continued to be embarrassed for another fifty-five years.

The Great Western lease document bound the company not to open any refreshment rooms or stopping places to enable passengers to procure refreshments other than the refreshment rooms at Swindon:

all trains carrying passengers – except passenger trains not under the control of the Great Western – which should pass Swindon station will stop for the refreshment of passengers for a reasonable period of about ten minutes and trains not under the control of the company should be induced to stop for the like purpose and the company has engaged not to do any act which should have an effect contrary to the above.

There is a touch of the highwayman in the phrase 'induced to stop' and indeed, Swindon refreshment rooms were the nearest thing to highway robbery on any railway. From the outset the Swindon refreshment rooms were so badly run that Messrs Rigby were in breach of their contract. The lease gave GWR directors the power to control quality and indeed, to annul the contract but they proved themselves incapable of doing anything to defend themselves from the ignominy of 'Swindleum Junction'.

On 18 December 1841 S&J Rigby sub-let the refreshment and hotel business for seven years to S.Y. Griffiths – who owned the 'Queen's Hotel' in Cheltenham. He paid the Rigbys £6,000 at once and a rent of £1,100 a year.[16]

Brunel made a comment about the poor service which reached the ears of the Manager, Mr Player, who passed it on to Mr Griffiths who had the cheek to write a letter of complaint to Brunel. Brunel's response was pithily perfect:

I assure you Mr Player was wrong in supposing that I thought you purchased inferior coffee. I did not think you had such a thing as coffee in the place. I am certain I have never tasted any. I have long since ceased to make complaints at Swindon. I avoid taking anything there if I can help it.[17]

A letter more typical of the period was written to the Chairman of the company by 'Mercator', a person who wrote many letters to *The Times* complaining about railways.

The position you occupy as Chairman of that important railway, the Great Western, induces me to address you personally on a matter of considerable importance to the public comfort and not to state facts which can by any possibility be unknown to you but to call your attention to them and to suggest a remedy.

Any attempt at discussion on the advantages or disadvantages of railways would be out of place. Unquestionably all other known modes of locomotion must yield to them wherever population and capital exist.

Yielding therefore to force majeure the individual who has to perform a journey takes his place on a train. If he has had much previous experience of travelling he very naturally makes contrast between what used to be and what is. If railroads are an addition to the general comfort of the community the advantages ought all to be on their side and this is the point on which I take the liberty to raise a question.

You sir, can doubtless enter into the old pleasures of the Stage Coach: the time it afforded for the contemplation of the beauties of nature – its contact with the real bustle of life – its course through a diversified population – through town and hamlet – its stoppages for refreshment – all these are gone – vanished into the air. Not even a glass of ale remains as a relic of the former system. The half hour for dinner, on wholesome, smoking, good old English fare has dwindled into the 'ten minutes delay' – for what?

Pork pies (probably stale)
Sausage rolls
Banbury cakes
A cup of coffee (not drinkable)

So choice a Bill of Fare for the traveller who has risen at six or seven in the morning and cannot get to his destination before a similar, or later hour in the evening. Pasty proof of the March of Improvement, truly!

To bring the question more into the form of narrative and for the sake of illustration, I beg to inform you that two friends and myself left Exeter last Monday morning and by posting [travelling by horse-drawn carriage] arrived at Taunton (where we were civilly asked by the check clerk why we did not arrive earlier) just in time for the train which reached Paddington at 7pm.

We were ready for the usual meal – which all who travel in First Class carriages expect at least once a day – when we arrived at Swindon where we disbursed seven shillings and six pence 'in no time' for pork pies and an indifferent bottle of malt liquor. One of my friends had an attack of indigestion on the road – and no wonder after such a meal. I believe I may state that we all heartily deprecated the dictum that placed such beggarly fare before the public and said to them 'Eat this or none – eat it up in less than ten minutes and run to the train when the bell rings – or you will be left behind with nobody to sympathise with your inconvenience.'

Who can doubt that such a system calls for a remedy. If half an hour was spared for a meal when coaches ran only 8 or 9 miles an hour why should an abridgement to a third of that time take place now that travelling is accelerated three-fold on your line?

The economy of time is made to excuse the giving one whatever sort of eatables those choose, who have been fortunate enough to obtain the purveyorship at Swindon. Granted there is no time for a hot dinner but would the man who travels from London to Exeter care whether he was six or seven hours on the road (he used to be twenty-four) provided his personal and necessary (I hope the last word will be fully understood) comforts were fully understood. Would the Public be likely to complain and if not

upon what possible grounds could the railway management object to the extension of time for resting – to whatever would give Ladies and Gentlemen and children all the facilities that they have already been accustomed to, in abatement of the inconvenience of travelling?

The truth is, Sir, your Swindon station is one of the best illustrations of monopoly that can anywhere be found. That there is no chance of any opposition tavern is well known and consequently it has not even occasion to hang out the sign of The FLEECE.

Your influential position as Chairman of the Great Western Railway must attach great weight to any opinion you may express on the necessity of a change in the time allowed for travellers for refreshments as well as in the quality of those refreshments. By carrying some improvement into effect the Great Western, not only by setting an example to Wolverton to which station these remarks equally apply, may gain 'Golden opinions from all sorts of people'.

In August 1848, Griffiths sold the lease to J.R. Philips. Philips' catering was even worse.

In November 1871 the Postmaster General made a contract with the GWR to run dedicated

Swindon Junction Station passenger/parcels statistics[18]

Year	No. of staff	Annual wage cost £	Total income of station £	Tickets sold	Season tickets	Goods £
1903	168	15803	42398	260276	nil	62525
1913	202	16668	45496	279162	nil	77484
1923	257	46308	79153	290890	341	183335
1929	254	46973	91138	302803	338	47382
1930	251	476301	90783	283953	327	44849
1933	239	42315	76714	235195	208	47286
1938	248	49281	80984	273442	490	60762

Swindon station, looking west from the Up platform, c. 1914.

for the benefit of Philips. Philips sued the company but the learned judge saw him off by ruling that these were trains outside the control of the Great Western. Philips sulked and sold the lease to Mr G. Moss in 1875. Moss was a reasonable person and the refreshment rooms at Swindon became 'one of the best in England'.[19] Good Mr Moss's high standards reduced his profits and in 1881 he sold to H.G. Lake, a traditionalist, who returned to the stale fare of 1843. It was this man to whom the GWR had to pay, in November 1895, the huge sum of £100,000 to get rid of him and take the room 'in house'. The first passenger train to run through Swindon non-stop was the 10.15am Paddington to Penzance – the 'Cornishman' on 1 October 1895. The abolition of the lease enabled the company to establish its splendid 'Hotels and Refreshment Division'.

mail trains, running to Post Office-dictated schedules, with a financial penalty on the GWR if time was not kept. These stopped only for five minutes at Swindon – and that was for GPO purposes not

Looking east from the west end Up platform line, c. 1914. There is a 'calling-on' arm below the home signal on the right. Later on this was removed and Rodbourne Lane's distant signal was the lowest arm on the post.

A lady passenger looks across at the devastation of the staff quarters of the station hotel on the Up platform. This was caused by a fire which broke out on the night of 27 March 1898. Swindon 'D' box is on the extreme left.

CHAPTER 10

Wootton Bassett

Wootton Bassett station opened for business when the railway was extended from Hay Lane to Chippenham on 31 May 1841.

It was built to one of the five standard designs Brunel had made for wayside stations, possibly even smaller than the one he chose for Shrivenham. The town of Wootton Bassett ranked only as 'wayside' – he had had a very draughty and generally uncomfortable night at the 'Cow and Candlesnuffers' in the town in early 1841.[1]

There could be no 'Great Western tradition' in 1841. That was something to be developed by the gentlemen directors and by those early employees who had realized that by joining the Great Western Railway they were entering into a new world where a disciplined, public-service[2] sense of responsibility for safety was needed rather than the rumbustious old ways of the stage coach. The 'Great Western tradition' was created, not by a supernatural being, not in six days but over many years by the directors and the growing understanding of their employees.

The locomotivemen and the policemen/switchmen had a hard school in which to learn and many fell out due, perhaps, to the hardship of their employment overwhelming their sense of responsibility: a policeman at Swindon was dismissed for deserting his signal and going to the pub at the foot of the embankment. Others managed to work for a year without being reported for any fault and thus to receive the annual bonus but they were definitely a minority in the early decades.

Wootton Bassett station was outstanding for the number of staff being reported and for the number of collisions and derailments. On 27 October 1841 Thomas Flynn, a switchman at the station was called to Paddington to be examined by the directors 'on a charge of serious inattention to Orders while the trains were working on one line in consequence of the slip in the incline embankment. This being proved, Flynn was dismissed from the company's service.'[3] Not paying attention during the working of the traffic of a double line over a single line is indeed a serious failing.

On 10 March 1842 Daniel Mereweather, switchman at the station, was seen by the Bristol Division superintendent to have 'neglected to give the proper signal to prevent the coming in of the 8.40 Up train the line at the station not being clear.' The very next day, Mereweather was standing before the directors to answer the charge. The minute concludes: 'The offence having been proved, Daniel Mereweather was fined 20/- to be paid over eight weeks.[4] Also on 10 March Mereweather was discovered by his sub-Inspector of Police, Thomas Burton, 'in the Lamp Room with a female'.

Not until the 16th did Mereweather, and witnesses Burton and porter John Matthew appear

Wootton Bassett goods shed and staff, c. 1885. There is mixed gauge track on the main line but only standard gauge on the sidings. The signal box is end-on to the track. A disc and crossbar signal is showing 'danger', conforming to the semaphore. Although close to the semaphore, this might be the Down distant signal. These ancient signals were commonly used in this mode in the first 10–15 years of 'absolute block' signalling. BROAD GAUGE SOCIETY

before the directors to answer this charge. The minute states: 'Examined as to the particulars of the incident when it appears that the female in question was a passenger about to proceed by the goods Train, directions having been given by a former superintendent to afford accommodation to Third Class passengers by admitting them to the Lamp Room. In the absence of sufficient evidence as to more direct impropriety of conduct, Mereweather received a strong admonition from the Chairman (of the Great Western Railway – Charles Russell MP) as to correcting his behaviour for the future.'

On 12 October 1842 a 'double headed' goods train was approaching Wootton Bassett on the Up line. The train driver was Mr Carter, the pilot engine driver, Mr Brown. Brown shut off steam when he saw the red light at Wootton Bassett but Carter had not seen the signal and did not shut off steam and so drove the train on to collide with a train of timber standing in the station. Carter was fined 20/- at 5/-- a week for his negligence and Brown was reprimanded for not sounding his brake whistle when he felt himself being pushed along.

Driver Hall was driving a goods train up Dauntsey bank on 9 December 1845. There was a freezing fog and the engine was cabless. Maybe the fog made the rails wet, maybe the load was just too great for the engine but it stalled. Driver Hall and his guard decided to divide the load and take the front half through to Wootton Bassett, there to stable it in a siding. A common enough occurrence. They 'put the front part away' and returned down the Up line the hill for the rest. Unfortunately fog signals – detonators – had not yet arrived on the GWR and the guard had not gone forward to meet the returning engine to warn driver Hall. The fog was thick and the engine, lacking anything but a handbrake, whacked into the wagons, damaging some of them.

Driver Hall appeared in front of the directors on 1 January 1846.[5] He pleaded 'fog' as an excuse but he was severely reprimanded for going so fast in dense fog and was fined 20/-. The guard should have been called in and reprimanded for not protecting his train but there is no record of that.

When the 6.30pm Bristol express arrived at Paddington on 9 August 1848, guard Moss reported that his train had run over some obstruction on the line at Wootton Bassett. The carriages were struck by something and bumped over something causing alarm to the passengers. An inspection of the line was made on the 10th but no evidence of an obstruction could be found. Policeman Balls who was on duty at Wootton Bassett at that time was called to meet the directors on the 11th. He denied that there had been any obstruction on the line but the directors felt certain that such must have been the case. Balls was consequently fined 5/- for neglect of duty. The minute of 11 August concludes:

> The decision of the directors being made known to him, Balls used very unbecoming language to the directors and violently assaulted Mr Burton, the Inspector of Police, in the Boardroom. He was at once dismissed from the Service and ordered to be taken before the Magistrate for the offence of assaulting Mr Burton.[6]

Fog was the very devil for steam footplatemen. Even in the days of powerful brakes, absolute block signalling and the Automatic Train Control they needed nerves of steel and an uncanny knowledge of the track to drive at express speed into foggy darkness, but in the early days all that driving in fog was next to suicidal.

There was thick fog between Swindon and Bristol on the night of 29 October 1862. The Swindon–Bristol mail train left Swindon six minutes late at 11.14pm. It consisted of an engine and three sorting vans, there were no passenger carriages. When it was 1¼ miles from Wootton Bassett a rod in the valve gear shattered and the driver brought the train to a stand. The guard believed that there was no train coming on the Down main for ninety minutes but even so he felt very exposed. He asked the driver if he could not get the train at walking speed into the protection of Wootton Bassett's signal. The driver agreed. The guard did not first go back to the rear to place detonating fog signals on the rail but got into his van and they went off at 5mph and came to a stand in the station with the red light of the station signal 60yd to the rear of the train. The signal could be seen for 1000yd on a clear night but on this night it was invisible at any distance because it was placed so high above ground. The other problem was that the station had the same signalling in 1862 as it had in 1841 – the company had not seen fit to provide it with a distant signal – to give early warning to a driver that there was a signal at 'danger' ahead.

At the station the guard discovered from the switchman/policeman that there was indeed a train behind him – the 2.10pm Paddington–Bristol goods which, had it been on time, would have long since passed Wootton Bassett. The guard was alarmed at the risk but did not want to walk back with detonators and asked the switchman to go. The switchman was reluctant because there was a 7.45pm Bristol–Paddington goods also long overdue which might turn up at any minute but he was persuaded to go. He collected some detonators and his hand lamp and set off. The mail train guard, thinking all was well, went to hold a lamp for the driver who had to take away the broken part so that the train could proceed to Chippenham on one cylinder.

The switchman put down a 'shot' at 500yd and at 950yd he put down three more, 10yd apart. He walked on and had gone 30yd when he heard the goods train approaching. It was 100 minutes late. He held up his hand lamp with the red light showing and he shouted a warning as it passed. Running over the three detonators caused the driver to open the sanding valve, call for the tender handbrake to be screwed down, put his engine into reverse with steam on and blow his brake whistle for the guard's handbrake to be applied.

The train consisted of forty-four heavily loaded wagons, the rails were slick with the fog and braking was, in spite of all that was done, not very effective. After 950yd of using every available technique of braking the goods hit the back of the mail at 10–12mph. The driver of the goods engine was thrown off the footplate and knocked about but no one else was hurt – the guard of the mail had had the sense to order the Post Office men out of the vans, two of which were damaged.

Captain Tyler, who investigated the incident recommended that a distant signal should be supplied to the rear of the Up and the Down station signals to be worked with a lever. He also suggested that a device to place detonating signals on the rail should be placed to the rear of the distant signal which would also have to be lever-operated.[7] The company forgot this sensible suggestion.

The Saturday night of 27 March 1867 was one of thick fog. At about 2.45am the Wootton Bassett switchman could hear a goods labouring up Dauntsey bank and he could hear by the exhaust beats that there was a banker at the rear. The train emerged out of the murky darkness and shuffled through the station. A couple of minutes later the bank engine pulled up at the platform ready to set back over the crossover and return to Chippenham.

The switchman worked the point capstan and waved the driver on. The engine was just joining the Down main when the 6.35pm goods, running at 35mph, came under the bridge and hit the engine. The switchman had either forgotten it and not placed his station signal to 'danger' or if it was at 'danger' the driver did not see it in the fog. The *Devizes & Wiltshire Gazette* stated:

Wootton Bassett station staff, c. 1895. The station building is one of Brunel's five standard designs. BROAD GAUGE SOCIETY

In 1863 the station staff were as follows:

- 1 Station Master   £110 per annum
- 2 Switchmen   23/- per week (£119 12s per annum)
- 2 Switchmen   22/- ditto (£114 8s ditto)
- 2 Police   17/- ditto
- 1 Porter   17/6d ditto
- 1 Porter   17/- ditto

NB 'The Station Master has been in the service for 17 years.' No 'Clerk' was included in the list, which is drawn from the GWR ledger (Rail 250/688).

The route was blocked with wreckage until 4pm Sunday. goods trains were suspended but passenger trains worked to both sides of the obstruction and passengers walked around or through the wreckage to board another set of coaches. Apart from the cross-over road which was smashed to pieces the track was little damaged. Both engines were thrown off the line, both seriously damaged. The engine of the Down train was bent and twisted in a curious manner and was half buried in the bankside. The trucks were broken to pieces by the shock and were piled around like so much loose timber. There were no casualties. Most remarkable was the survival of the driver of the 6.35 Paddington. He was found buried in debris, still standing on his footplate, scratched and bruised but otherwise unhurt.[8]

The GWR obtained an Act of Parliament on 7 August 1896 to construct the 'South Wales and Bristol Direct' railway from Wootton Bassett station to Filton and Patchway connecting with the existing Bristol–Severn Tunnel railway. This was just one of several heavily engineered, new main line railways the company was undertaking: this one cost £986,084 in gold sovereigns.[9] The old station at Wootton Bassett was demolished and replaced by one built to the simple 'New Line' design. The new railway opened throughout to goods traffic on 1 May 1903 and to passenger trains 1 July. The station remained a 'wayside' place with a service of 'local' passenger trains running between Swindon and Bristol over the old and the new main lines.

The station was closed for all purposes from 5 December 1964.

Wootton Bassett passenger/parcels statistics[10]

Year	No. of staff	Annual wage cost £	Total income of station £	Tickets sold	Season tickets	Goods £
1903	22	1463	16378	15263	nil	8014
1913	19	1479	16187	47131	nil	6557
1923	22	3898	27523	38782	599	10669
1929	22	3504	26191	42580	792	7579
1930	22	3515	24208	42000	792	8980
1933	20	3223	41828	32112	611	6868
1938	22	3673	31189	42770	959	6235

The Vale Signal Boxes

An Introduction

On 11 April 1872 the company informed the Board of Trade that the installation of the mixed gauge had been completed between Didcot and Swindon and invited BoT Inspection. Captain Tyler was sent to inspect. He found a railway equipped with the equipment installed at the opening of the line in 1840, the newest technology being Brunel's 1842 signalling system: time interval, disc and crossbar signals, points worked by the hand-turned capstan, the switchman holding the capstan lever while the train was passing over the points.

Captain Tyler reported:

I have been with Mr Tyrrell and the Oficers of the Great Western Railway Company over the portion of line herein referred to between Didcot and Swindon. The gauge is now mixed between those places and the narrow gauge is nearly complete for the sidings as well as the main lines though further work has yet to be done, especially in some of the sidings.

The most important place on this length and in some respects on the Great Western system, is the Swindon Junction and yard. The very extensive works in connection with that Yard, and the lines and sidings in it and about it have grown from time to time during a series of years into a condition of complication.

They require general re-arrangement and improvement with the introduction of modern appliances for working points and signals with locking apparatus. At Didcot and the other stations similar improvements are also required although to a lesser degree. I understand that they are in contemplation and I recommend that they should be carried out at all points at which there are connections with the main lines with as little delay as possible.

The 'modern appliances' referred to signal boxes containing the electric telegraph used to maintain a definite distance between trains, and 'locking machines' to interlock the levers which worked the points with the signals. The railway through the Vale was equipped with signal boxes during 1874. They were brought into use on 31 March 1874.[1] The principle of the 1874 'Block' signalling was that the line was always clear unless stated otherwise. The normal display of the telegraph instruments was 'Line Clear' and the normal position of the signals was to show 'All Right'. When a train passed signal-man 'A' he put his signals to 'danger' and sent one beat on the electric bell to 'B' if the train was carrying passengers and two beats if it was a goods train. He released the white topped 'Line Clear' key on his telegraph instrument and pegged down the red key. This caused the display on his instrument to change to 'Train on Line'.

The signalman at 'B' repeated back to 'A' the bell signal and pegged down the red key on his instrument working to 'A'. When the train passed 'B' and the signalman saw its tail lamp, he sent 3 beats to 'A', unpegged his red key and at once pegged down the white 'Line Clear' key on his instrument. The signalman at 'A' could now lower his signal arms with the levers.

The sequence of signal boxes through the Vale in 1874 was: Steventon Station, 56 miles 45 chains; Steventon Causeway Crossing, 56 miles 72 chains; Wantage Road, 60 miles 25 chains; Challow, 62 miles 49 chains; Uffington, 66 miles 42 chains; Knighton Crossing, 69 miles 0 chains; Ashbury Crossing, 71 miles 5 chains; Shrivenham, 71 miles 56 chains; Marston Crossing, 74 miles 15 chains; Swindon boxes 'A', 76 miles 29 chains; 'B'; 'C'; 'D'; Rodbourne Lane; Hay Lane; Wootton Bassett. This is the full list taken from the 1874 GWR Signalling Regulations.[2] The distances are measured from the buffers at Paddington station.

The March 1874 signalling regulation was changed in November 1885 to the effect that the line was now always to be considered 'blocked' until the signalman in advance – towards whom the train was going – agreed that the line was clear at his place. That is still the system in 2014 where mechanical signalling is in use. A 'signal box' accommodates a signalman and the electrical instruments with which he communicates to the signal boxes on each side. A signalman has the power to accept or refuse to allow a train to approach his signal box.

A signal box is defined as a 'block post' because of the signalman's true function – to block or clear the line. A 'ground frame' could look like a signal box – as one did at Steventon – but it was not a 'block post'. It was a shelter for the crossing keeper and his equipment: he could not accept or refuse to accept the approach of a train. He had a gate wheel and two levers, one to lock/unlock the pedestrian gates and another to lock/unlock the main gates and at some places he had levers to control the arms of signals worked from the station signal box.

The original, 1874, signal boxes between Steventon and Wootton Bassett were in one of two types: the GWR's small red-brick building with outside stairs, pitched, slated roof and plain gables; or a Saxby & Farmer timber building under a slated, hipped, roof. The railway between Didcot and Swindon was a double track. One track in each direction had to accommodate express passenger trains travelling at 50–60mph and goods trains with a speed of 20–25mph. The low speed was due to the absence of brakes on the wagons and to the primitive lubrication of axle bearings. A grease which the railwaymen called 'yellow fat' was used. The rotation of the axle created warmth which melted the grease to some extent so that it 'ran' around the bearing but if the axle rotated to quickly the melted grease could not keep up with the metal, overheating of unlubricated metal occurred, heat caused the grease to ignite and burn away, then the white metal bearing to melt and the cast iron beneath the melted metal sawed through the axle. It was about 1900 before the Great Western began to fit wagons with oil-lubricated axle bearings

By 1875 'refuge sidings' of varying lengths had been installed – mostly on the Up side – at Shrivenham, Uffington, Challow, Wantage Road and Steventon. On the Down side there were, in 1875, refuge sidings only at Wantage Road and Challow.[3] When Foxhall Junction let a Down loose-coupled, unbraked goods train leave – and most goods trains for the next fifty years would be loose-coupled and unbraked – it had to move forward very slowly to ease the couplings out taut on thirty or forty wagons without making a tug that might snap the chain, then get the train up to 20–25mph, travel 7 miles to Wantage Road, and then to stop as carefully as they started and reverse off the main line. Seven miles would take 17 minutes – pass to pass – but if starting, stopping and reversing has to be allowed for, a train of that type would need 27 minutes to get in clear of the main line at Wantage without delaying the following passenger train. Such time-consuming methods restricted the number of trains that could be run.

Steventon

In 1874 Steventon Station box was built into the sloping ramp at the west end of the Up platform. It accommodated a fourteen-lever frame four of which were 'spare'. One lever is described on the 1883 plan as working a 'wire lock'. This gave the Steventon Station signalman the ability to lock/unlock the gate lock lever at Stocks Lane ground frame, 264yd further west.[1] The 1883 plan of signalling shows the Down distant signal for Steventon was 1,220yd to the east of the signal box but shows no Up distant worked or slotted by Station box.

A 'distant' signal arm horizontal indicated that the 'Stop' signal ahead was at 'danger' and so the driver should start to brake. 'Slotting' was a mechanical contrivance to allow one signalman to control another signalman's signal – both signalmen had to pull their lever for the signal arm to drop to show 'All Right', either man putting his lever back to 'danger' replaced the signal arm to 'danger'.

The next signal box westwards was Causeway Crossing on the Up side of the line, on the east of the crossing. It had eight levers, of which one was spare. Causeway's Up distant signal was 1,069yd west of the signal box and applied to both signal boxes. Causeway's Up home signal was 'slotted' from Steventon Station box making it the latter's home signal too. Causeway's Down home was slotted by Station box as the latter's Down advanced starting signal. The signalling plan[2] gives no indication of Causeway having a Down distant so Steventon Station box Down distant applied to both boxes. Because of the two level crossings it seems likely that all the signals remained at 'danger' until there was a need to clear them.

The Up refuge worked from Steventon Station box extended so far west that it crossed the Stocks Lane, which must have been very annoying for local people when a goods train stood there waiting for a passage eastwards.

A Down refuge siding was brought into use, worked from Causeway, in late 1882 or January 1883. The access points for this were immediately east of the level crossing and gave a function to the erstwhile spare lever. The blade of the points moved a rotating signal on the ground to tell the driver the points were set for him to leave – and of course the Causeway signalman could shout to the driver from his window.

West of Causeway, at 57 miles 5 chains, was Berrycroft Crossing. A building was provided here for the crossing keeper. On the 1875 survey its appearance caused the surveyor to mark it as

A fine view of the original design for GWR signal boxes, c. 1925. The station master is in the nearest upper window, the signalman at the other end and porters ranged along the ramp. PENDON MUSEUM

Steventon Stocks Lane gates and signal box from the Up side, 1964.
PENDON MUSEUM

Steventon Stocks Lane, 1962. During re-wiring of the GWR block signalling instruments. The interlocking lever for Causeway Crossing is reversed. It had a blue upper and a brown lower part. The electric gong communicating with Causeway Crossing is on the 'block shelf' above the gate wheel. Extreme right of the shelf is the GWR 1947 permissive block instrument for the Up goods loop. The indicator shows two trains are in the loop.

'signal box' on the plan.[3] It must be supposed that Causeway box had a control over Berrycroft gates.

In 1883 Stocks Lane ground frame was given signalling instruments to become a block post. There were now three signal boxes in a fraction over a mile with Stocks Lane having slots on Causeway's Up and Station box's Down 'stop' signals, including Station box's Down home, on the east side of the road bridge. Stocks lane gates, when swung across the tracks, were several feet apart with enough space for inside cylinder tank engines, unable to stop at the home signal, to pass through without hitting the gates: that condition remained until the gates were replaced by automatic half barriers.

In December 1891 a Down refuge siding was installed with the connection to the Down main situated immediately east of the main road bridge. The points and siding starting signal were worked from Steventon Station box but Stocks Lane had a slotting control on the siding starting signal.[4] The Down refuge worked from Causeway Crossing was taken up as a result of the new refuge.

In July 1907 an Up goods running loop, 2½ miles long, was brought into use from the east end of Steventon station to Foxhall Junction, Didcot, with Milton signal box intervening. The facing points into the loop at Steventon were immediately east of the bridge. There was a 'directing' signal to the loop, on the outer home as well as the usual 'main to loop' signal just to the rear of the points. The extra points, facing point bolt and signals required a larger lever frame and a 27-lever frame was installed in Steventon Station box of which five were spare.[5]

A goods loop was worked under 'permissive' regulations allowing any number of trains – not conveying passengers – to occupy the loop simultaneously. A special signalling instrument was provided in each signal box enabling the signalmen to keep a tally of how many trains were in the loop.

In July 1921, the eight-lever Causeway Crossing box dating from 1874 was demolished and replaced by a larger, wooden signal box containing twenty-seven levers, There was no obvious reason for this but perhaps the directors were still hoping to quadruple the route. The new Causeway Crossing box was a wooden building 22ft long by 11ft front to back with he operating floor 8ft above the rails. In March 1928, because of the invention of the Westinghouse hand generator for signal boxes, the GWR was able to reduce significantly its signalling costs. Steventon Station box was demolished, the 1921 Causeway Crossing box was taken to Stocks Lane and was given a 36 lever frame while the 1884 Stocks Lane box went to Causeway which was reduced to the status of ground frame.[6]

Stocks Lane box now controlled the whole station layout. The box was 836yd from the entrance and exit points for the goods loops up at the main road bridge but with the hand generator – the 'hurdy-gurdy' as the man called it – and with track circuiting to show the position of the trains, those points were operated by electric motors using electricity generated by the signalman winding the 'hurdy-gurdy' in Stocks Lane signal box. The output generated by the signalman was registered by an ammeter fixed above the generator. Because of the length of cable to the points the 'hurdy-gurdy' handle was stiff and heavy to turn.

Stocks Lane was a busy box. The signalman had the Up and Down goods trains to consider to keep the lines clear for the passenger trains, and he had Causeway and Berrycroft Crossings to supervise. The gate lock lever in Causeway was mechanically bolted from Stocks Lane but eventually the locking lever was made to operate an electric lock in Causeway. Communication between the two crossing ground frames and Stocks Lane was by electric bells in the ground frames and a coiled metal gong in Stocks Lane signal box. The bell signals between Stocks Lane and Causeway were:

- Call attention   1 beat
- May crossing be used*   1–3–1

Highworth station building, c. 1960.
GREAT WESTERN TRUST

Steventon Causeway ground frame in 1965. The ancient Causeway leads off on the left. PENDON MUSEUM

- Crossing clear gates in normal position   2–1
- Train approaching   1–2–1
- Close gates train signalled   3–2–1
- Obstruction danger   6
- Cancel last signal   3–5
- Testing bells   16

The crossing was not to be used until the bell signal marked * had been repeated by the signalman. If permission to use the crossing was not given at once, the crossing keeper had to send the signal at short intervals.

At Steventon Berrycroft Crossing (57 miles 5 chains) the calls were:

- May crossing be used?   2–4
- Crossing may be used   4–4
- Crossing clear after use   2–1
- Crossing cannot be used   6
- Test   16

The crossings were not to be released after 'Line Clear' had been obtained for a Down train or an Up train.[7]

Berrycroft Crossing was closed between 1948 and 1960, and no official records survive.

Reading 'panel' electric control room took over the operation of points and their signals – as far west as Steventon on 27 September 1964 but Stocks Lane and Causeway Crossing ground frames remained in use. Lifting barriers replaced the gates at Stocks Lane on 1 October 1972. On 27 January 1974 Stocks Lane ground frame was closed and the barriers were then controlled from Causeway Crossing ground frame using a CCTV for observation and an electric switch. Because of CCTV the crossing was floodlit at night. Causeway also controlled the colour-light signals approaching the crossings on the Up and Down line. On 15 November 1975, the old signal box turned ground frame building at Causeway Crossing was closed and its work transferred to an ugly 'Portakabin' on the other side of the lane from the old building.

Lockinge

The first signal box to carry this name was a erected in late 1903 or early 1904. It was a wooden cabin at 58 miles 51 chains, 12ft 6in × 10ft, containing four levers.[1] This was a 'break section' box, carefully placed almost exactly halfway between Steventon Causeway Crossing and Wantage Road, thus halving the time either signalman had to wait to hear 'train out of section' and thus be able to ask 'is line clear?' for the next train.

The 'Hanney Depot' – as it was known locally – was a military supply place that began life in about 1915 to supply horse fodder and saddlery. The entrance to it was on the Hanney–Steventon road, north of the railway and from there its buildings

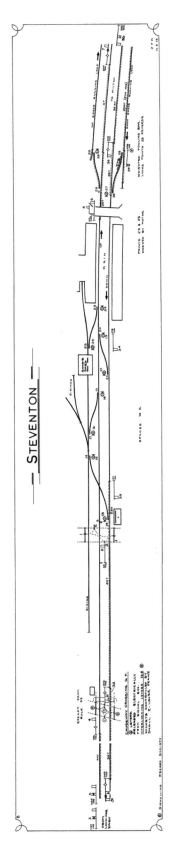

STEVENTON

Steventon, 1928–65.

were laid out in two rows southwards to the railway line. In 1940 it became rail connected and the signal boxes controlling access to it were called 'Lockinge': the village of Lockinge was three miles away to the south. Two loops for goods trains were laid on the north side of the main line with two signal boxes, 943yd apart, to control them. Lockinge East, at 57 miles 55 chains, was brought into use on 25 August 1940 and Lockinge West, at 58 miles 18 chains, on 15 September 1940. Both signal boxes were red-brick buildings with plain gables under a slated roof with operating floors, 25 × 12ft, 8ft above rail level. East box had thirty-five levers and west box twenty-one working levers in a frame for thirty-six.[2]

In a GWR Report into the problems of operating the line between Steventon and Swindon, written in January 1947, there is this:

> It should be noted that the loops at Lockinge, although shown on page 352 of Appendix to the No. 4 Service Time Table, are not available. These loops are within Government property, the gates are closed across them and are only opened when the Depot is being shunted.[3]

Shottesbrooke signal box, a 'break section' box from 1899, east of Twyford, c. 1958. With the exception of accommodating eight levers, it is identical to the original Lockinge. PETER BARLOW

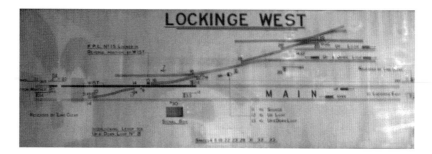

Lockinge West, 1940–60. Though of poor quality, this is the only known view of either boxes' track diagram and has only recently come to notice.

The 1948 BR(WR) No. 4 Sectional Appendix states that:

Lockinge War Department sidings are situated on the Up side between Steventon and Wantage Road. During daylight the gate at the east end will be kept open with a policeman on duty and the gate at the west end will be kept closed. When a train requires to call at the depot or it becomes necessary for emergency purposes to use the loops the signalman will telephone the Depot police who will unlock the gate. Fifteen minutes notice must be given to the police and Swindon Control will inform the signalman of any train requiring to call at the Depot.

The signal box diagram for the West box does not show the gates across the loops.

On 10 June 1947 pannier tank engine, No. 7404 had worked the 2.20pm Swindon to Challow goods. It then set out to run 'light' to Didcot but at 5.12pm became a total failure at the fifty-eighth mile post, between Lockinge East and West boxes. One of the

A 'Hall' with a Down, 'D' headcode, partly vacuum-braked goods, passing Lockinge East in 1955. This view shows perfectly how a Down train can hide the tail lamp of an Up train. PETER BARLOW

two connecting rods driving the crank axle had become disconnected. Both Lockinge boxes were switched out so the fireman walked two miles back to Wantage Road to report the obstructed line and to phone the foreman at Didcot shed to ask for assistance. He arranged for a fitter and a 'light engine' to carry him out to Lockinge and while he did that, the station masters at Steventon and Wantage Road organized temporary single line working over the Down main. That was brought into use at 5.36pm. The light engine with fitter arrived at Lockinge at 5.54pm. The fitter was dropped off to remove the connecting rod and the engine continued to Wantage Road where it crossed over to the Up line and came back to Lockinge. When the very heavy connecting rod had been dismantled and removed the light engine propelled it to Steventon and Didcot. Normal working was resumed at 8.23pm.[4]

Lockinge East box was taken out of use on 16 August 1950. Access to the depot was still available by the West box but on 8 January 1960, all connections into the depot at the West box were removed.[5] The signal box survived, although it was hardly ever switched in and it was taken out of use on 15 December 1963.

Wantage Road

The first signal box here was erected on the Up side, east of the bridge. There is no record for the size of the original lever frame. However, from the 1875 survey it is clear that four levers were required for points and six for signals, so probably there were 10 working levers and maybe four spares, as at Steventon.

On 11 November 1907 an Up goods loop was brought into use from Challow to Wantage Road.[1] The track met end-on with the existing Up refuge siding so no extra levers were required in Wantage Road signal box.

At 11.4pm on 15 December 1914 signalman Geater at Challow 'asked the road' to Wantage, on the Up goods loop, for a freight train. It had started from Stoke Gifford yard, bound for Brentford and consisted of 47 wagons and a 24-ton brake van, hauled by a Dean 'Standard goods', the number of which is not given in the Board of Trade Report. Driver Fry was in charge. He went into the loop at about 15mph, which was a bit brisk. The gradient was very slightly falling at 1 in 754. Driver Fry knew he'd be 'inside' for a while so he told his mate to get his sandwiches

Wantage Road preparations for quadrupling showing the c. 1847 goods shed, the 1915 signal box and the, as yet unopened, 1933 signal box beyond.

out and the two of them sat and talked and ate, the train pushing them past Circourt box at about 'a bit over 10mph' according to driver Fry's very honest testimony. There was no distant signal on the loop, to warn that they approaching for Wantage Road. Driver Fry said he took Wantage Road's Up main distant as his marker for the approach to the end of the loop. But he and his mate were relaxed, it was dark and they had been at work for 6 hours. Driver Fry never noticed the distant signal and it was only when he looked up and saw the red light of Wantage Road's Up main home that he realized he had missed the distant. His testimony reads:

> It was not until my engine was reaching the home signal that I realized the mistake I had made. I estimate our speed at 8mph. I shouted to my mate (to screw down the handbrake) and applied the steam brake. My train did not come to a stand before running into the buffer stops, still doing 8mph. I did not see my mate again after I saw him applying the handbrake. As soon as I saw that we were running into the buffer stops I caught hold of the water scoop handle and when we came to a stand I was hanging out over the right hand side of the tender. My engine turned over on its left side but the tender did not turn over. I then proceeded to the signal box and told the signalman that both lines were blocked. I then went back to look for my mate and found him pinned beneath the cab of the engine. I think he was already dead.

Driver Fry had to take the blame for the crash and thus the death of his fireman – who is not named in the report.[2]

In December 1915 a new signal box was brought into use. It was the Great Western's most handsome design in smooth red bricks with blue bricks around locking room windows and at the corners of the walls. There was a hip-gabled, slated roof. It was 25ft long, 11ft wide and the floor was 6ft above rail level. It contained a frame of thirty-five levers, although the track layout remained as it had been in 1875.[3]

That handsome box remained in use until 7 October 1932 when it was replaced by a new design in connection with the quadrupling of the line to Challow. This was a steel-framed building with concrete block walls. It had a floor about 35ft long, 12ft wide and 12ft above rail level. It contained a 61-lever frame.[4] When a train for the West Curve at Didcot was approaching the signal box the driver would give two blasts on the ordinary whistle and one on the brake whistle – a 'crow' whistle – and the Wantage signalman would advise Foxhall Junction signalman.

6003 'King George IV' with the 3.55pm Paddington–Swansea passing Wantage Road at about 5pm on 25 May 1961. PETER HAY

5005 'Manorbier Castle' with thirteen or fourteen coaches passing Wantage Road's Up distant signal, 2,400yd from the signal box on 27 August 1955. The two Denchworth road bridges are visible behind. D.M.C. HEPBURNE-SCOTT/RAIL ARCHIVE STEPHENSON 1613

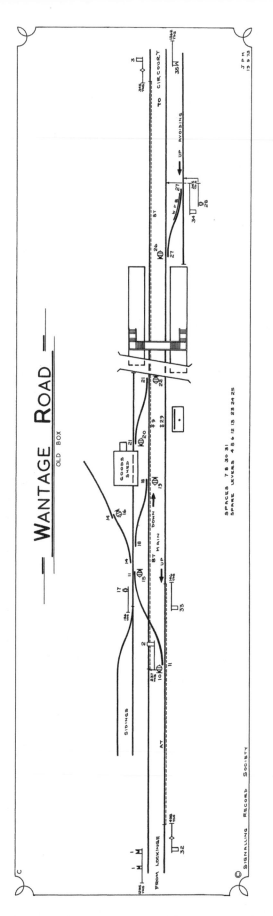

Wantage Road, 1907–32.

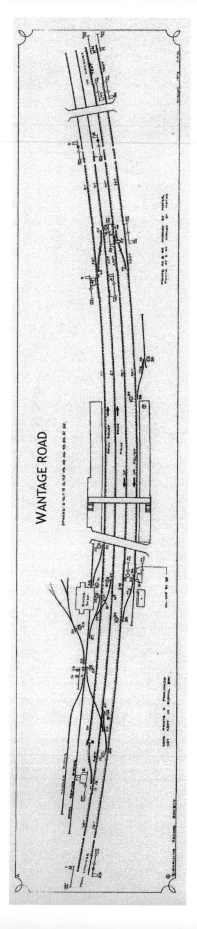

Wantage Road, 1932–65.

The signal box was taken out of use on 30 May 1965 with the extension of power signalling from Reading.

Circourt Crossing

In 1904 an all-timber 'break section' box with this name, was erected on the Up side of the line at 62 miles 49 chains. The signal box was a wooden building with a floor 12ft 6in × 10ft and held four levers.[1]

Circourt Crossing signalmen worked a distant and home signal on each of the two tracks. Because it had no connections between the loop and main lines it did not need inspecting and does not appear in the reports on the new goods loop. The signal box stood beside the lane leading from the Wantage–Faringdon main road to Denchworth and if the crossing had gates, the signalman opened them by hand. On 27 March 1906, the company informed the Board of Trade that work had begun on laying an Up goods loop on the upside from Challow to Wantage and on 26 July 1907 the company wrote again to say that the work was complete and ready for inspection.[2]

On 18 July 1915 a new Circourt Crossing signal box was opened with twenty-five levers.[3] This was to operate facing points installed Up main to Up loop with exit points from the loop back onto the Up main. This did not need twenty-five levers but twenty-five would have been required if a loop off the Down main had been installed. These two points and their associated signalling were removed soon after the end of the First World War, reverting Circourt to a four-lever break section box.

The signal box was taken out of use in May 1953, replaced by colour-light distant and home signals operated from Challow and Wantage Road on the Up and Down lines respectively.[4]

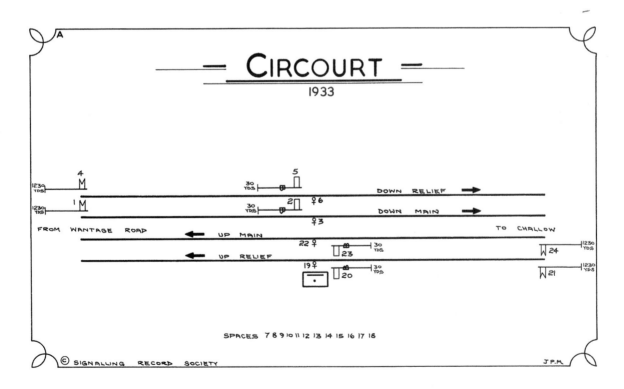

Circourt, 1932–54.

Challow

The 1874 signal box here was sited on the Down side at about the 63 mile 73 chain point. It was the standard GWR design for a small signal box and contained eighteen levers to work a layout very little changed since the station ceased to be a temporary terminus. A trailing crossover from Down main to Up main and goods shed was added in 1842 and before 1875 Up and Down refuge sidings were installed. In 1904 Challow began working with Circourt box and from November 1907 the signalman had the Up goods running loop to Wantage Road, to use to get goods trains out of the way of passenger trains.

In 1932 work began on quadrupling from Challow to Wantage Road and as a consequence of this building a new station. The old Up main became the new Up relief line and the old Down main became the new Up main. The Up relief diverged from the Up main at about 64 miles 20 chains and the Down relief merged with the Down main at the sixty-fourth mile post. The new platforms flanked the relief lines and were the length of

Challow signal box interior looking east in 1962. It was gloriously immaculate with blacked cast iron, lever handles burnished to a silver-smooth gleam, brasses flashing in the sun and the bare floorboards behind the levers scrubbed with a brush and yellow soap with hot water. This work was done during the relatively quiet Sunday day shifts.

Challow signal box at night in 1963. The left-hand end of the instrument shelf. The first five dials are BR standard signal arm indicators for the Up main and Circourt signals, the next four for the Up relief line. The Up main signals are cleared for a train. RON PRICE

The signalling bells and instruments and track diagram in 1963. The occupation of each length of track by a train is registered by the aluminum ball falling backwards out of sight. A very unusual piece of kit, it was known as 'All Balls'. All woodwork polished with 'Mansion' polish. RON PRICE

The right-hand end of the shelf with a mixture of BR and GWR signal arm repeaters (1963). RON PRICE

twelve eight-wheel coaches. A few yards east of the east end of the platforms power-operated points connected the Up and Down platform lines with the Up or the Down mains.

A new signal box was provided on the Down side at 63 miles 76 chains. It was built using a steel framework to hold concrete blocks. The roof had hipped gables and the tiles were hung by their

The 10.55am Paddington–Pembroke Dock. Timed to cover 133½ miles to Newport non-stop in 130 minutes with only eight coaches, the fireman had a pleasant job – and in this case seems to have overdone it somewhat. The author rode the footplate of this train to Pembroke Dock in 1962.

corners, in a 'diamond' pattern. The steps up to the operating room were within the building. Having reached this, one saw a gleamingly polished interior. The linoleum floor covering reflected perfectly the cream and brown lockers and the silver-handled levers. The floor was about 40ft long by 13ft front to back and stood 12–13ft above rail level. The levers were numbered to sixty-three but with twelve spaces. The layout extended from the Up distant, 1,381yd to the west, to the Down main and relief distants, 1,772yd to the east.[1] The latter was fixed at caution. The Down main distant – which remained a GWR wooden signal to the end – was worked by an electric motor by 1944.[2]

On the Up line at Challow the distant was 1,010yd to the rear of the 'home', on the Down line there was 1,128yd braking distance to the home. The Up distant was replaced with a colour-light, 2,228yd from the signal box, on 1 September 1958, giving a braking distance to the home of 1,466yd.[3]

Trains scheduled non-stop through Swindon but which required to take water at Swindon gave a

The 8am Cheltenham, non-stop Kemble–Paddington timed to average 60mph over the 91 miles.

No. 6112 leaving Challow westwards at 7.45am after putting off some coal wagons into Challow siding in 1962.

long 'crow' on the brake whistle as they approached Challow and the signalman then contacted Swindon West box.

In 1923 the 2.30pm Cheltenham was inaugurated to run from Swindon to Paddington non-stop, 77¼ miles in 75 minutes. Minutes were cut from the schedule as the years passed until, in 1932, the 2.40pm Cheltenham (it had been re-timed) had a schedule of 65 minutes. The train was a bright spot in 'Depression' years and became known to the public as the Cheltenham Flyer. In 1932, with the ultimate schedule in place, the GWR recognized this with a 'head board' displaying that title, which was placed on the top lamp bracket in front of the engine's chimney.

Naturally the train had a privileged 'path' – other trains were timed to be out of its way – and the signalmen viewed it as sacred. The Old Oak Common footplate crews vied with each other in the 'Cheltenham Flyer Stakes' to beat 65 minutes and the ultimate record was made by driver Street and fireman Sherer working No. 5005 'Tregenna Castle' when they took the train from Swindon to Paddington in 56 minutes, 42 seconds. Steam engines only go as fast as the skill of their crew can make them go – it isn't merely a matter of turning a handle – and that required skilful, intuitive firing and driving.

In 1935 the 4.30pm Bristol–Paddington was inaugurated to mark the GWR's centenary year and

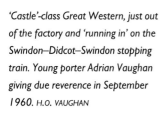

'Castle'-class Great Western, just out of the factory and 'running in' on the Swindon–Didcot–Swindon stopping train. Young porter Adrian Vaughan giving due reverence in September 1960. H.O. VAUGHAN

officially named the 'Bristolian', although it did not carry a headboard. Both of these trains came through the Vale at 90+mph in order to keep time.

This Swindon–Paddington non-stop run became a 'Blue Riband' challenge to the footplatemen. An old Swindon driver – who was a fireman at Swindon long before the war – told the author that he and his mate had taken a train of empty coaches from Swindon to Old Oak Common, late on a Sunday evening. They were confident they would have a clear path at that time of night and they set out to beat the record. They had a 'City'-class 4–4–0 and it was a beautiful moonlit night. He said that, had they been bound for Paddington, they would have made it in 55 minutes. He recalled fondly for me the moonlight flashing on the 'City's' side rods and the grins he and his mate exchanged as they topped 90mph up through Steventon and the Thames Valley. In his lucky mind's eye, it was all like yesterday.

As a schoolboy volunteer in Challow box the author regularly 'got the road' for the steam-hauled 'Bristolian' and pulled the levers for it. But times changed: there were no more stopping passenger trains and the number of goods trains was dwindling. On 4 May 1965 the Up and Down relief lines were taken out of use and Challow box was reduced to a mere block post. On 30 May 1965 Challow box, the author's pride and joy, was taken out of use.

Uffington

Uffington's original signal box was a very tall structure on the Up side, just west of the level crossing of the Fernham–Uffington lane. Judging by what can be seen of it in the picture of the broad gauge 'Rover'-class engine, it was a wooden, Saxby & Farmer production. It held a 28-lever frame.[1]

The station had seen many fatalities. In May 1893 porter Jennings went up the Down main starting signal post to re-light the oil lamp. The post was 30ft tall at the edge of a 15ft embankment. There were no guard rails around the lampman's platform on which Jennings had to stand. He slipped and fell to his death. So the lamp was not re-lit but

Heavy freight engine No. 3863, passing the closed signal box at Challow on 15 August 1965 at 55–60mph. 25mph was their usual speed because of the unbraked weight they hauled.

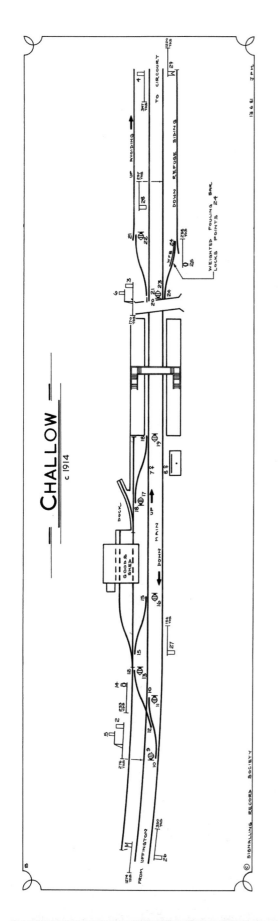

Challow, 1907–32.

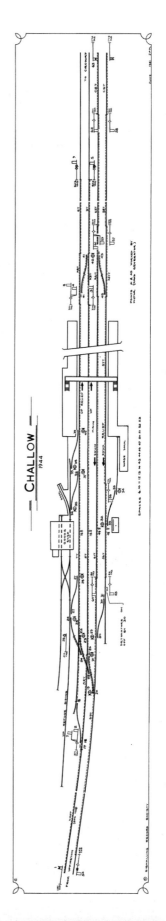

Challow, 1932–65.

A broad gauge 'Rover'-class engine brings an express past Uffington circa 1890. The roof of the 1874 signal box is in the smoke. The glimpse of the roofing shows it was a Saxby & Farmer building. The Faringdon branch train is in the background and a double disc and crossbar signal.

the signalman took no action. He did not wonder where Jennings was. At 6am, when the signalman was relieved by the early turn man, the absence of Jennings was mentioned and the fresh signalman went to the signal and found Jennings lying on the grass.

The coroner's jury asked why there was no lamp winding-up gear on such a tall post to which the company replied: 'We only fit that on posts over 30ft tall.'

The level crossing proved to be particularly fatal. This was hardly surprising since the road crossed three sidings and the main line. There were gates on both sides of the five tracks, but the farm carts had to come inside the gates in order to work in the goods shed or at the milk dock.

In 1891 a carter drove his horse hauling a cart containing milk churns to the milk dock at the station, off-loaded and, leaving his horse by the dock went across to the 'Junction' pub. After a boring half-hour the horse decided he wanted to fetch his carter and go home. He plodded slowly onto the level crossing where he was immediately smashed to bits.

On 1 April 1893, the Old Berks hounds were hunting and their quarry led them to the station. The riders had to stop at the closed gates and were

milling about there when a cart horse, left unattended further back along the lane, thoroughly excited by the passing of the hunt, and, still attached to his cart, came charging into the throng. Mr Jefferies was thrown off his horse and killed.

In 1894 a group of four men were killed on the crossing and, shortly after this, a happy young lad called Gerald Ritchings was rolling a milk churn along on its bottom rim, carelessly walked down the platform ramp and into the path of a train. At this point the Berkshire coroner wrote a letter to the GWR – and surely reported also to the Board of Trade – that he was thoroughly fed up with investigating deaths at the crossing 'hairbreadth escapes are also talked about freely – the crossing is generally dangerous' and asked what the directors intended to do about it. They replied in Olympian Great Western fashion that they 'did not care to comment on airy generalities' and asked for details. As for local gossip, that was no concern of theirs. They were willing to build an underbridge but it would flood each winter. They could not build an overbridge because that would require the road to be diverted onto land not owned by the company.[2]

The Board of Trade held an inquiry at the station on 26 July 1894. The subsequent report opened quite crossly with the words 'These complaints are

Uffington looking east soon after the completion of rebuilding, about 1899.
NATIONAL MONUMENTS RECORD

Uffington looking east off the bridge, 1964. DON LOVELOCK

No. 5978 'Bodinnick Hall' freewheels to a stand with the Up 'stopper', Alfie White keeping an eye on Richard Casserley, c. 1958. R.M. CASSERLEY

entirely reasonable and in no way exaggerated.' The outcome was that the directors had to obtain an Act of Parliament for the compulsory purchase of the land on which to built the embankments up to a bridge. The locals were angry about the dangerous crossing but one of them was not angry enough to sell a small plot of land without being forced to do so under an Act of Parliament, costing the company dear.

A full-scale reorganization of Uffington station now took place. The works commenced in January 1897. The new bridge was a 'bow and string' construction, assembled in riveted steel and erected by the contractor Jackman of Slough. It had to cross a 90ft gap but being built 'on the skew' was 109ft long. In October some of Jackman's men went on strike and got drunk, and one of his blacksmiths, repairing a rail wagon owned by Jackman, had his head crushed between the closing buffers of two wagons.

The platforms were lengthened. A new signal box of forty-seven levers was built on the Up platform, east of the station building to control an enlarged layout. The original goods shed by the station was demolished. An Up refuge was laid to the west of the bridge and a siding to a goods loading platform on which was built a brick, 'lock-up' goods store. Baulking cutting sides were excavated to enable two storage sidings, 250yd long, to be laid on the Up side and a refuge siding for forty-two wagons, engine and van, on the Down side. All this work was carried out by GWR staff: one of them was killed by a passing train. All the works were complete by January 1898.

Faringdon signal box accommodated six levers, the electric telegraph instrument and signalling bell. The little building had a floor space 7ft 1in × 5ft 1in.[3] The Down distant signal for Faringdon was 'Fixed at caution' and there was a Down home and an Up starting signal. As far as passenger trains were concerned there were two facing points. The first set would, if reversed, divert left to the engine shed, the next set would turn a train right, into the goods yard. The signal box was in use from 1882 to 1933.

The first three months of 1947 were exceptionally cold with frequent heavy snow storms. The Vale of the White Horse was particularly badly

Looking west on the Up platform to show the branch line, the coal merchant's office – by then the signal lineman's workshop – and the red and yellow brickwork of the station master's house, by this time housing the lineman Bob Tanner and his wife, Stella. GREAT WESTERN TRUST

A Didcot-based '56'-class 0-6-2 tank, which had brought the 'Didcot Fly' here, simmering on the branch while the guard and footplatemen rest from their heavy labours on the milk dock. They await the return of the Faringdon goods. GREAT WESTERN TRUST

RIGHT: The branch fortuitously fell steeply downhill giving the small tank engines which normally worked the branch a good 'run' at the long steep bank ahead. Taken in 1961 from the lamp platform of the Up branch distant signal.

affected by the final blizzard from 3 to 6 March when the Faringdon and Highworth branches were truly buried in snow.

On 17 October 1950 an event took place between Knighton Crossing and Uffington which might be unique in the history of GWR and Western Region. The author was told the outline of events by signalman Elwyn Richards at Uffington in 1961, and later met the widow of the ganger who saved the day and received a certificate for his meritorious service.[4]

The goods arriving at Faringdon. The engine came bunker first from Swindon and 'ran round' at Uffington to be chimney first to Faringdon; the fireman has omitted to remove what was the headlamp from the bunker. Things were very relaxed on the branch: the author had several trips over the line as the driver. JIM BROWN

Faringdon goods yard with No. 1410, an 0-4-2 tank engine carrying out the shunting and a group of Oxford University Railway Society (OURS) chaps wandering out, c. 1955. PETER BARLOW

LEFT: Faringdon station with a GWR diesel rail car on tour. Mr Hale, station master of Shrivenham and Faringdon on the platform, 24 April 1955. RAIL ARCHIVE STEPHENSON 1503

ABOVE: The Up branch home signal at Uffington – seen here in 1961 – was erected 50yd to the rear of the site of a Brunellian double disc and crossbar between 1892 and 1896.

LEFT: The view from the guard's van on the first mile out of Faringdon with the return trip to Uffington, c. 1955. And extra van was provided to give the OURS members a safe place in which to ride. Requests for privileges to the local BR (WR) office, such as Swindon, were met with friendly acquiescence and cooperation. PETER BARLOW

The train conveying OURS having arrived at Uffington, the engine 'cuts off and runs round' in order to propel the wagons into Baulking sidings, c. 1955. PETER BARLOW

The train was the 4.55am Fishguard to Paddington boat train, fourteen coaches long, hauled by the four-month-old 7032 'Denbigh Castle'. The fourteenth was a slip coach, No. 7696, put on at Cardiff to be detached on the approach to Didcot. No. 7696 was of 1906 vintage, a Churchward 'Toplight', otherwise known, because of its ten inset doors, one for each compartment all along its 70ft length, as a 'concertina' coach. The heavy train rolled into Swindon at 10.22am. As this was the last stop before the slipping point, the vacuum brake flexible pipes between the thirteenth and fourteenth carriages had self-sealing valves attached and then the brake pipes locked together. The coupling shackle of the thirteenth coach was put over the hinged draw hook of the slip coach and the wedge was pushed forwards by the guard's 'slipping lever' to hold the hook in position. The train left at 10.29.

The 'slip guard', was Frank Snell. He was 51 and had been a railwayman since 1915. He was selected to be a passenger train guard in 1941 and had been a slip coach guard for two years. He booked on duty that day at 5.45am and worked two round trips with a passenger train to Highworth and

back before taking charge of the slip coach and its twenty-five passengers. At the inquiry Snell stated that the train started at 10.29am, and he sat down. As the train passed Highworth Junction box, one mile from start, he noticed that he had 'not secured the slipping lever in the running position'. He had not pushed the slipping lever fully forwards so that the lever latch had not dropped down into its slot in the quadrant and therefore the wedge driven by the lever was not fully engaged above the tip of the hinged slip hook.

Snell said he 'held the lever in position' until, exhausted, he had to let go of it, the wedge came away from the tip of the hook, the coach was slipped and came to a stand at the 68¼ mile post, between Knighton Crossing and Uffington.

Guard Snell grabbed detonators, got down onto the track and hurried back towards Knighton Crossing to place the detonators and protect the coach. The train had passed ganger Brown walking towards Uffington. He was at the 68½ mile post when he saw the slip coach come to stand. He immediately turned back towards Knighton Crossing signal box. After 440yd he placed three

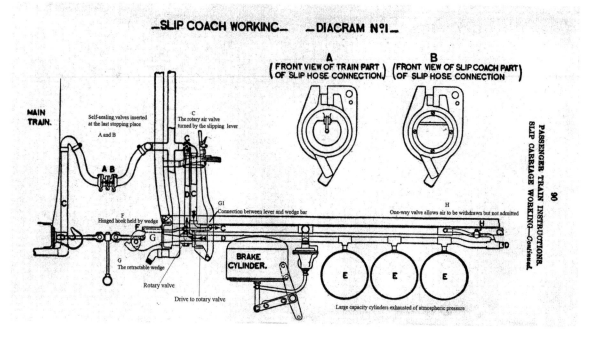

The slipping lever retracts the wedge (G) between the hinged draw hook (F) and the casting above the wedge. When pulled backwards or pushed forwards – to the central 'stop' – it turns the rotary air valve (C).

detonators on the rail and hurried on to warn the Knighton signalman.

The Fishguard passed Uffington at 10.43. The signalman there, Elwyn Richards, the most steady and reliable man, seeing the double red tail lamp, and forgetting that this indicated that the slip coach was missing, gave 'train out of section' to Knighton and accepted the 10.25am Swindon–Reading stopping passenger train. This passed Knighton Crossing at about 65mph, according to driver Herbert George's statement, at 10.46am. with all signals cleared. The engine exploded ganger Brown's detonators, and driver George at once applied his brakes. The engine ran over Snell's set of detonators and stopped half a mile from the first braking application. The slip coach was about ¼ mile ahead.

Guard Snell then arrived from where he had been standing by his detonators with a red flag and instructed George to go onto the slip coach, couple up and push it into Uffington. This was done and the coach and train arrived there at 11.15. Passengers from the slip coach were put into the stopping train, the slip coach was shunted into Baulking sidings and by 11.25 the 10.25 Swindon went on its way.

Guard Snell's explanation was accepted by the inquiry, although it was pointed out to him that, seeing the position of the lever at Highworth Junction, it would have been more sensible to slip the coach within the protection of signals than try to hang on to it for another 23 miles. No-one was punished and ganger Brown got his certificate for good railway work.

During February and March 1962, a new lever frame was installed to work a new layout: the Down refuge siding was taken out of use and Up and Down goods loops were installed, situated to the west of the Fernham road overbridge. These held a maximum of seventy wagons plus engine and van. The Faringdon branch was still in operation, worked from the new frame. Both main line distant signals were renewed as colour-lights.[5] The Faringdon branch was closed for ever on 1 July 1963.

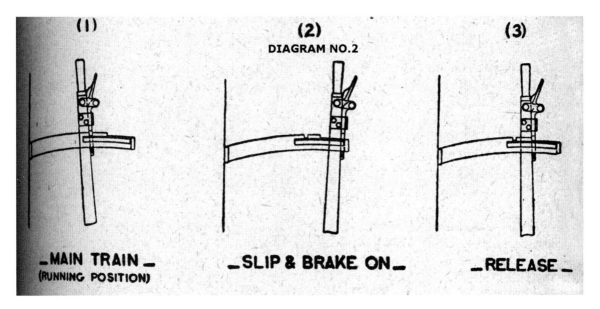

(1)   **(2)**
DIAGRAM NO.2   **(3)**

MAIN TRAIN
(RUNNING POSITION)

SLIP & BRAKE ON

RELEASE

To slip the coach the slip guard presses the lever latch against the lever handle and pulls the lever backwards, towards himself thus withdrawing the wedge and the hook, no longer obstructed, falls, releasing the shackle of the main train.

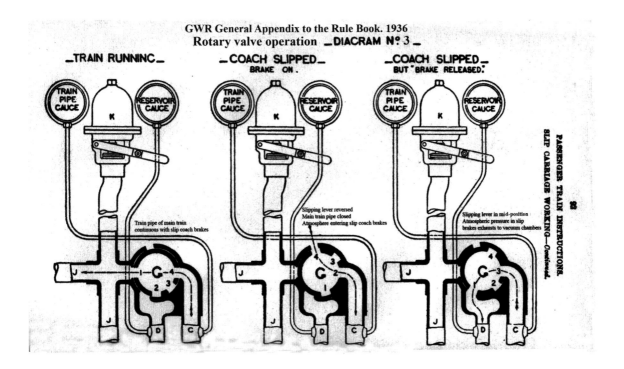

GWR General Appendix to the Rule Book. 1936
Rotary valve operation _DIAGRAM Nº 3 _

TRAIN RUNNING

COACH SLIPPED
BRAKE ON.

COACH SLIPPED
BUT "BRAKE RELEASED."

TRAIN PIPE GAUGE   K   RESERVOIR GAUGE

Train pipe of main train continuous with slip coach brakes

Slipping lever reversed
Main train pipe closed
Atmosphere entering slip coach brakes

Slipping lever in mid-position
Atmospheric pressure in slip
brakes exhausts to vacuum chambers

PASSENGER TRAIN INSTRUCTIONS.
SLIP CARRIAGE WORKING—*Continued.*

By pulling the lever fully back, the rotary valve is turned and admits atmospheric pressure – about 14psi – to the pipe leading to the brake cylinder in which resides the brake piston. There is a vacuum throughout the brake cylinder so that when atmospheric pressure enters to cylinder to brake piston is lifted and applies the brakes to the wheels. A one-way valve prevents atmosphere entering the space above the piston. The slip guard allows the coach to fall back a safe distance from the main train and then pushes the lever to the mid-way stop. This rotates the valve and connects the atmospheric pressure in the lower brake cylinder to the cubic capacity of the 'vacuum reservoir' beneath the coach whereupon the brakes are released. The vacuum reservoirs were large enough to enable the guard to apply and release the brakes seven times.

As from 3.30pm on 30 May 1965, Uffington signal box began to work with the new power signalling 'panel' at Reading to the east and the mechanical signalling westwards. By stages, the mechanical signalling to the west of Uffington was abolished until Uffington was working with Highworth Junction. Uffington signal box was abolished on 3 March 1968.

Knighton Crossing

The level crossing of the road from Uffington, Woolstone and Compton Beauchamp crossed the railway exactly at the 69 mile post and headed north towards Longcot and Shrivenham. When the railway opened the crossing was called Longcot. It was well used and was provided with two policemen/crossing keepers – on 12-hour shifts and quite probably one man doing 24 hours on a Sunday to allow the other a day off. The crossing was 1¼ miles from Longcot, two miles from Compton Beauchamp and even further to Uffington/Woolstone so these men, wherever they found a lodging, would have had a tedious walk to and from work. The directors quickly came to the conclusion that having a man on the crossing all night was unnecessary and therefore expensive. At a meeting of the General Traffic Committee of 15 September 1841: 'the necessity of a night policeman at Longcot Road gates was

considered and instructions given to ascertain what would be the cost of a cottage there for the permanent residence of a policeman.'[1] The directors envisaged that one man could do a day shift and then be on call whenever someone wanted the gates open between 6pm and 6am. If he was married his wife could get up and open the gates. Given what is known of crossing keepers' cottage arrangements within living memory, that was certainly the idea – however, no action was taken.

On 16 March 1842 Constable Tickner, policeman at Longcot gates, was not present to open them for a Mr Wilson of Shrivenham, thereby causing that gentleman much delay. Wilson wrote to the company and Tickner was summoned to Paddington to explain himself. His defence was that he had gone to get a sheep hurdle to block up a gap in the railway fence to prevent lambs from getting onto the line. His story was corroborated by Inspector Wells but the directors were not impressed and, for absenting himself from his post, Tickner was fined two shillings and sixpence a week for four weeks. His wages would have been fifteen or sixteen shillings a week.[2]

The idea of a cottage re-surfaced on 5 January 1863 when the general manager reported to the directors that it would be cheaper by £1,000 a year to build houses at all level crossings for either the crossing policeman or a platelayer so that the night

Seen here in 1960, Knighton Crossing signal box in the heart of the Vale, with the wonderful White Horse Hill behind, stood precisely 69 miles from Paddington and precisely 300ft above sea level. The embankment from Uffington, rising at 7ft per mile, briefly meets natural ground here and continues through a shallow cutting.
H.O. VAUGHAN

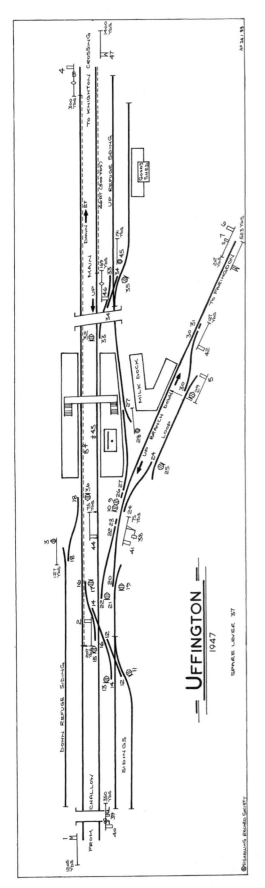

Uffington, 1896–1951.

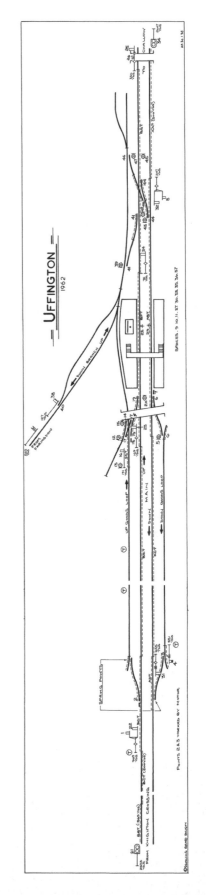

Uffington, 1962–63.

On a misty April day in 1964, the young chap appears to be willing the signalman to ask him in. ROD BLENCOWE.

crossing keeper could be dispensed with.[3] The cottage at Longcot gates was built, it is shown on the 1875 survey. It was on the Up side of the line, gable end-on to the east side of the lane. In plan it is shown as a larger rectangle with a narrower rectangle continuing eastwards. There was a privy at the far end of the garden.

The signal box was listed at the head of the 1874 signalling regulations as 'Knighton Crossing'. It probably had six levers to work a distant and home in each direction and two levers to lock/unlock the

road and pedestrian gates. It never had a crossover. The signal box was not built to the original 1874 design but to the second style, introduced in 1875.[4]

On 12 December 1904 an Up goods running loop was brought into use from Shrivenham to Knighton Crossing and a frame of ten levers was installed to operate the locks on the level crossing gates, the new signal and points coming out of the loop, and the new Up and Down main starting signals.[5] There never was a ground signal to reverse into the loop from the Up main.

1960, 400yd south of the crossing and the only dwelling in sight of the crossing, a 16th-century cottage on the lane to Woolstone. Surely a navvy or two got lodgings here in the vast loneliness of this place during the building of the line. H.O. VAUGHAN

Signalman Nelson Edwards looks out at the photographer. Nelson started his career on the Midland & South Western Junction Railway about 1912. He had some remarkable recollections of that struggling company. HUGH DAVIES COLLECTION

The company's intention was to continue the goods loop to the Up refuge siding at Uffington. The bridge taking the railway over the Wilts & Berks Canal at the 68 mile 50 chain point was extended northwards to enable the loop to continue eastwards over the remains of the canal but the work was not carried out.[6]

Knighton box never had electricity, piped water or lavatory. Drinking water was delivered daily in a small can with a brass tap, carried on the buffer beam of the Up and Down Swindon–Faringdon goods.

The signal box was taken out of use on 14 November 1966, replaced by the very objectionable automatic half barriers. On 8 March 1974 the road was diverted in an underpass through the embankment a few yards east of the crossing. This had been planned before 1875 because the land for that is shown on the 1875 survey.

An Up express passes a lowly freight train 'waiting the road' in the goods loop at Knighton in 1954. If a goods train driver was to misjudge his halt at the signal, the points would direct him and the engine onto 'Olde England'. E.J. NUTTY

This happened on a foggy evening in October 1964. The engine's steam regulator was faulty, it would not fully shut off so the driver, free-wheeling along the loop, opened the cylinder steam cocks to prevent the steam working on the pistons. So he had no forward vision at all and was trusting his judgement. He almost got away with it. *E.J. NUTTY*

After two weeks an attempt was made to raise the engine using hydraulic jacks. This failed, leaving a larger hole for the engine to sink into. 48610, an ex-LMS freight engine, was a regular visitor to the line at that time. *E.J. NUTTY*

BELOW LEFT: The engine was there for so long, it became a monument to the end of an era. *RON PRICE*

BELOW: After lying another TWO weeks, two 45-ton steam cranes hoisted it. The front end was embedded to such an extent that the force of the 'lift' drove the nearest crane downwards and the track it stood on had to be repaired. *E.J. NUTTY*

Ashbury Crossing

Ashbury Crossing was brought into use in 1874 at 71 miles 5 chains. The number of levers is not known but eight with six working is most likely. The style of the building is not known but supposedly it was the original GWR type. The crossing gates were not long enough to meet between the Up and Down tracks. There was a crossing keeper's cottage on the Down side at the west side of the road. It had an original ground plan identical to the one at Knighton Crossing but with a later addition on the south side. It was there before 1875 and was still there in 1930.

A Down goods loop was brought into use on 23 March 1903.[1] The facing points were just west of the level crossing and ran to an end-on junction with the old refuge siding at Shrivenham. The addition of the loop required a new frame of twelve levers in the old box. On 12 December 1904 an Up goods loop was installed from Shrivenham to Knighton.[2] Ashbury Crossing had no control over this but there

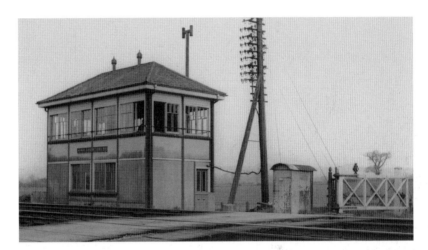

Ashbury Crossing signal box, north face. ROD BLENCOWE

No. 4915 'Condover Hall', coming out of the Up relief line from Shrivenham and joining the Up main at Ashbury Crossing with the 1.21pm Bath–Paddington stopping train. The Down goods loop is well shown in this view on 26 May 1958. J.C. HOLE

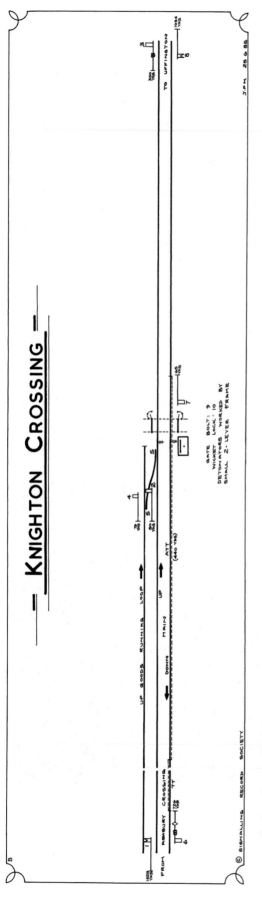

Knighton Crossing, 1904–66.

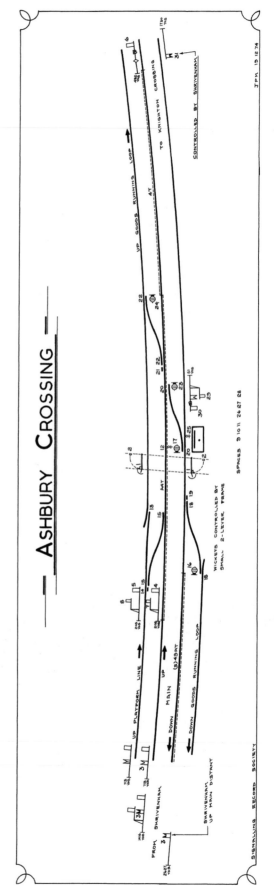

Ashbury Crossing, 1933–66.

must have been a bell in the Ashbury box repeating the codes sent between Shrivenham and Knighton in order for the Ashbury signalman to have the gates shut across the road in time for the train to pass.

In 1934 large changes came about: the track from just east of Shrivenham station to Ashbury Crossing was quadrupled. The enlarged layout required a new signal box at Ashbury. This was built to the standard design as at Wantage Road and Challow. The platform line at Shrivenham was extended east to merge into the Up goods loop at Ashbury with facing points to take passenger trains onto the Up main, just west of the crossing. Another set of facing points from the Up main to the Up goods loop, just east of the crossing – and a main to main crossover were also added. There were thirty-one levers: twenty-three working and six spare.

In April 1944 two 'ambulance sidings' were laid down on the Up side of the line immediately west of the level crossing. The six spare levers were brought into use to work the additional layout. The

sidings were a transfer point to road vehicles. The rail connections to the 'ambulance sidings' were removed on 11 December 1949.[3] Ashbury signal box was taken out of use on 14 November 1966.[4]

Shrivenham

The first signal box at Shrivenham was erected in 1874 and was built to the GWR first standard design.[1] In 1874 the main Shrivenham–Ashbury road crossed the railway on the level at the foot of the eastern end of the platform ramps, too far away to be supervised by the signalman. No crossing ground frame building is shown on the 1875 survey but it must be supposed that a gateman was provided and there must have been some form of communication between him and the signalman. According to the 1875 two-chain survey, Shrivenham station tracks and signals required a maximum of ten levers so it is probable that the signal box contained a twelve-lever frame. This would be similar to the other wayside station signal

A 'Castle' on a Down express passing Shrivenham's Down main home and main to platform line signal on 26 May 1958. The Down goods loop starting signal is alongside, behind the coaches and Ashbury box can be faintly seen on the left beside the telegraph pole. J.C. HOLE

boxes east of Shrivenham. But the history of signal boxes at Shrivenham between 1874 and 1934 is shrouded in mystery.

In 1883 the company attempted to bring into use a Down refuge siding with points trailing into the Down main a few yards east of the platform ends. The rails crossed the Shrivenham–Ashbury road. Colonel Yolland for the Board of Trade refused permission for this to be used because reversing a train over a public road constituted a danger to the public and was thus illegal under the Railways Act of 1863. Eventually the road was carried over the line on a 'horseshoe' bridge and the Down refuge came into use sometime between 1890 and 1898.[2]

The siding required two extra levers and my supposition that there were two spares covers that: one exit signal lever and one point lever – a ground signal operated by the movement of the point blades would have been all that was required to allow the train to commence reversing.

On 23 March 1903 a Down goods loop was installed between Ashbury Crossing and Shrivenham station.[2] The new track from Ashbury Crossing joined end-on with the old Down refuge siding so no extra levers were needed in Shrivenham box.

On 12 December 1904, an Up goods running loop was brought into use from the east end of Shrivenham station to Knighton Crossing.[3] Major Pringle for the Board of Trade inspected both installations on 1 May 1905.[4] He reported that the new connection to the Up loop was 'worked from Shrivenham Station box with an old frame of twenty-one levers of which two are spare'. Was this 'old frame' the 1874 frame unnecessarily large, or was a larger signal box and frame supplied in 1883 – when the supposed old frame would have done the job? The Signalling Record Society Register shows a new frame of twenty-nine levers being installed at Shrivenham in 1909, five years after the enlarged layout had been brought into use. The SRS does not make such statements lightly. By no means all of the Board of Trade signalling inspection reports have survived to the present day.

In 1931–32 the Down side of Shrivenham station was demolished and rebuilt as a four-track station. The Up and Down platforms were served by loops off the Up and Down main lines. Goods trains could enter either platform loop. Up goods trains could then either be turned out at the opposite end of Shrivenham station or continue on to Ashbury to be turned out or go on to Knighton Crossing. During the Second World War and especially in 1944, the Up loop between Ashbury and Knighton would be lined with goods trains queuing for a 'path' eastwards. Footplatemen were liable to spend an entire 8-hour shift sitting on their engine and not leave the loop.

A new signal box was required at Shrivenham for the quadrupled layout and a new standard building as at Ashbury was erected and brought into use on 18 September 1932.[5] It contained a frame of fifty levers: forty were working, including four detonator placer levers, the rest were spares.[6]

On 15 January 1936 signalman Bill Head was on night shift in Shrivenham box and signalman Jefferies was at Ashbury Crossing. It was a very

Looking west along the Down platform at Shrivenham in 1934–5. The brand new signal box, after the same pattern as Challow, can just be seen in the distance. It was not then equipped with a flush lavatory or piped water. PENDON MUSEUM

frosty night, pitch dark and misty. At 5.8am an Up coal train entered the section to Shrivenham from Marston Crossing. The train consisted of fifty-three loaded wagons with a 24-ton, six-wheeled brake van at the rear, in which a guard was riding, hauled by a heavy freight engine, No. 2802. The wagons had no brakes, their weight was approximately 1,100 tons and driver Davis, with only his 108 tons of engine and tender to brake the train, was driving very carefully down the slight gradient at 20mph.

The draw hook of the forty-eighth wagon fell off 990yd east of Marston Crossing signal box. The rear part very gradually slowed so the gap between it and the first portion grew wider. Guard Chandler had served as an infantryman in the First World War. He had successively been gassed, then wounded, and finally taken prisoner in March 1918. He had no way of knowing that his van and the last five wagons were now detached from the train. As the wheel beats slowed he thought they were stopping for Shrivenham home signal although he admitted he did not notice the absence of ringing buffers as the wagons closed up. Only when his van had stopped did he go outside to look. He saw Shrivenham signal box lights some way ahead and when he looked backwards he saw the twin headlamps of an approaching express. He jumped down from his van and ran between the two tracks

towards it but even if he had put down detonators it was too close for that warning to have been any use.

In Shrivenham box signalman Head watched the coal train trundle slowly by because it was being turned into the Up loop at Ashbury to clear the line for the express. Head sent 'Train entering section' to Ashbury at 5.14am. As the coal train passed, a train of empty milk tanks went by on the Down main. That would obscure the tail lights of the Up goods so he watched for the single red lamp at the back of the empty stock and then turned to look for the three red lights of the Up goods. The van was not there, but standing outside his home signal, so there were no tail lamps to see – but he sent the fatal 'Train out of section' signal to Marston Crossing at 5.18am. He told the inquiry: 'I could swear I saw what I took to be a tail lamp on the Up goods' and so he sent 'Train out of section' to Marston at 5.18am.

Signalman Jefferies at Ashbury Crossing, half a mile further on, also sent 'Train out of section' for the goods at 5.18am. This might, in fact, have been 5.19 – signal box clocks were not synchronized and the time actually written in the train register can vary by half a minute each side of the clock figure. Jefferies had not seen any tail lamps – he said he had his back to the window taking a phone call as it passed. But if he had not seen the tail lamps – for whatever reason – he ought not to have sent 'Train out of section'.

No. 5914 'Ripon Hall', only three years old, stands at Shrivenham Down platform with a train of empty milk churns in 1934. Unloading local churns and waiting for an express to pass down the main line. The Brunel station shows nicely in this view.

Four minutes elapsed before the Up express passed Marston, at 5.22, four minutes in which one of them could have had second thoughts about the tail lamps. The collision occurred at about 5.24½am. The engine, No. 6007 'King William III', was hauling the train at about 55mph. It derailed, turned onto its right side and came to rest lying between the rails of the Down main. GWR locomotives were all designed to be driven from the right-hand side of the cab. Driver Starr, of Old Oak Common shed, was fatally impaled on the handles of the engine's reversing screw and ten passengers were seriously injured. Fireman Cozens got away with minor cuts and bruises.[7]

Bill Head seems not to have received any punishment and continued as signalman at Shrivenham until his retirement years later, and, according to those who knew him, every day he was haunted by the knowledge of what he had done. Jefferies seems to have been considered more culpable than Head because he had had an unobstructed view of the rear of the train from 30ft. Jefferies was sent to be signalman at the single line station at Radstock. Men who worked with him and who worked with me later on, said he was an addicted gambler. He gambled that night at Ashbury and driver Starr lost.

Shrivenham signal box had no flushing lavatory and no piped water, from its opening until 1946 when a proper lavatory, tap water and a wash basin was installed.[8] It was taken out of use on 5 June 1966[9] (see page 118).

The Marston Boxes

Marston Crossing box was opened in 1874 on the Up side of the line at at 74 miles 15 chains. It was merely a 'break section' box, with a distant, home signal in each direction but it had control of the gates across a 'public highway'. On 7 February 1883 Col. Yolland for the Board of Trade came to inspect the recently installed Up and Down refuge sidings and associated signal interlocking. He reported an eight-lever frame with no spares. The plan accompanying his report shows a distant, home and starting signal in each direction plus two levers to operate the Up and Down siding points. The entrance and exit signals for each siding worked with the movement of the point blades. The ground plan of the signal box shown on the 1883 plan strongly suggests that it was one of the original GWR small brick signal boxes.[1]

In 1920 the Great Western intended to create a very large 'hump' shunting yard at Marston.[2] Long-distance freight for Bristol and the West, South Wales and Gloucester coming from East Anglia, the Midlands, North and Kent/Sussex, was to be sent to a hump shunting yard at Iver, and marshalled for Marston. The railway between Didcot and Marston was to be quadrupled throughout. The following year the government forced the 'grouping' of railways. The GWR was, thereby, encumbered with huge expenses to absorb sixty small railways, not necessarily in the best condition after the First World War, and the Marston scheme, which was well into the planning stage, died.

Marston Crossing box carried on its modest duties until 1942 when a marshalling yard was constructed between 73 miles 61 chains and 74 miles 14 chains, requiring two signal boxes: Marston Crossing East and West, the latter being more or less on the site of the original box. The layout here consisted of – apart from the sorting sidings – the Up and Down mains and Up and Down goods loops and two reception lines for trains to put off/take on traffic. The Up goods loop was situated on the Down side, entailing two inconvenient crossings of the Down main line one at the West box and another at the East end.

Marston West box, with thirty-seven levers, was brought into use on 7 June 1942, but full operation of the marshalling yard did not begin until the East box, with thirty levers, was opened on 29 June.[3] After the war the yard remained busy with Down fish trains and Down milk empty tanker trains. The former came in from East Anglia behind LNER engines, the latter from London Wood Lane or Kensington and were re-marshalled for Gloucester, South Wales and the West of England. On 15 July 1962 the Up goods loop was converted into a second Down loop and an Up goods loop was laid on the Up side.[4] Marston East box was closed on 13 February 1966 and the West box on 14 November of that year.[5]

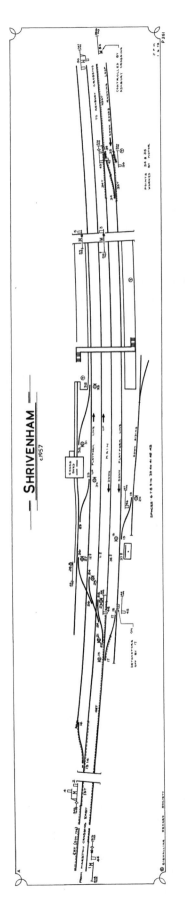

Shrivenham, 1933–66.

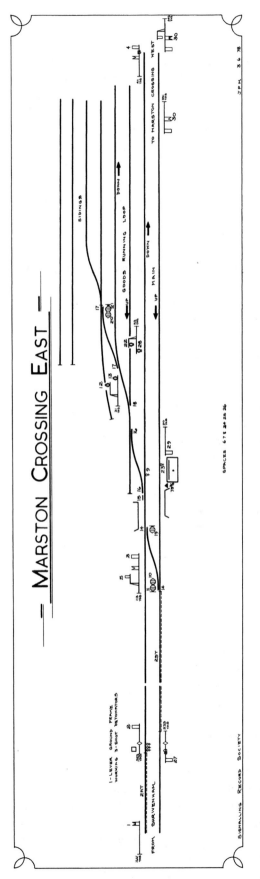

Marston Crossing East, 1942–63.

LEFT: *Looking south on South Marston lane, towards the Oxford–Swindon road. Fine old trees, a beautiful train, the promise of a comfortable old pub: Roye England's picture of a Vale idyll. The future Marston East box, in the violent time to come, was built just to the right of the bridge.* PENDON MUSEUM

Marston Crossing East box beside the parapet of the bridge with some fine signals, 8 September 1953. PENDON MUSEUM

BELOW: *Roye photographed Marston East Down main home and Down main to goods loop home with Marston West's distant below on 8 September 1953.* PENDON MUSEUM

Signals within goods loops and sidings carried a white ring on the red arm. The signal is lowered for a left turn onto the Down goods loop, the left-hand arm lowered would route to the Down siding. In pre-war GWR days, this 'siding' arm would have been thinner and shorter. Marston West box beyond. 8 September 1953. PENDON MUSEUM
BELOW: *Marston West box.*

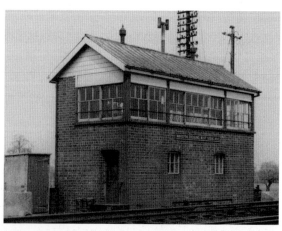

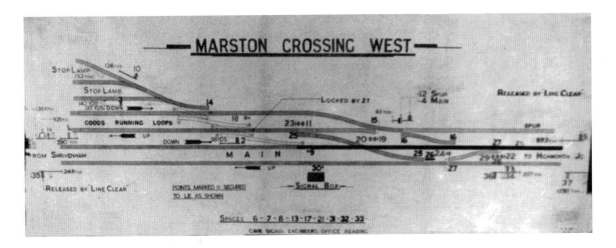

The track diagram showing the Up goods loop situated on the Down side in 1960.

BELOW: Ex-LNER 2-6-2 No. 60845 passing Marston West on the Down main in 1953. It was working a trials special and deeply impressing the Swindon drawing office people behind the front shelter and in the dynamometer car with its tremendous power. The author's friend E.J. Nutty was part of the research and development team on board.

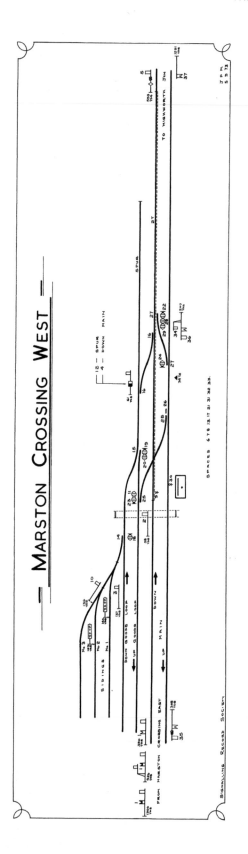

Marston Crossing West, 1942–63.

The Highworth Branch

The Highworth branch started life with signal boxes at Stratton, 1 mile 24 chains from Highworth Junction and at Hannington 4 miles 32 chains from the Junction. Stanton station, between these two, was just a platform beside the signal track. Highworth station never had a signal box but had two ground frames unlocked by a key on the train staff. Stratton box was closed on 4 June 1906 and Hannington box closed on 27 June 1910.[1] The sidings Hannington and Stratton had gained were accessed from 'south' and 'north' ground frames unlocked by the train staff. The necessities of the First World War brought Stanton Wood siding into use to admit trains to carry away felled timber. A large factory for the manufacture of explosives and for filling artillery shells was opened ¼ mile along the branch from Highworth Junction on 18 February 1917. This was – in that dreadful year – mightily busy and the junction into the factory required a signal box with ten levers. This closed with the factory on 28 July 1919.[2]

During the Second World War, the first 2 miles and 10 chains of the branch from Highworth Junction, gave access to various large works with miles of sidings. The electric train token system was then introduced on 17 February 1942 to regulate the passage of trains with a new signal box with an eleven-lever frame called Kingsdown Road working with Highworth Junction. Beyond that the wooden train staff was in use to Highworth station. Access to these factory sites was by various ground frames unlocked by the ETT. This gave access to the South Marston branch leading to the Spitfire factory. After the war more sidings worked from ground frames were added including the huge complex serving the Pressed Steel company's car body works.

Kingsdown Road signal box was taken out of use on 6 August 1962.[3]

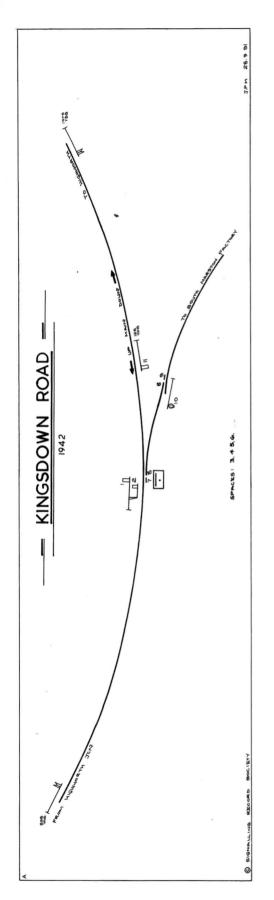

Kingsdown Road, 1942–62.

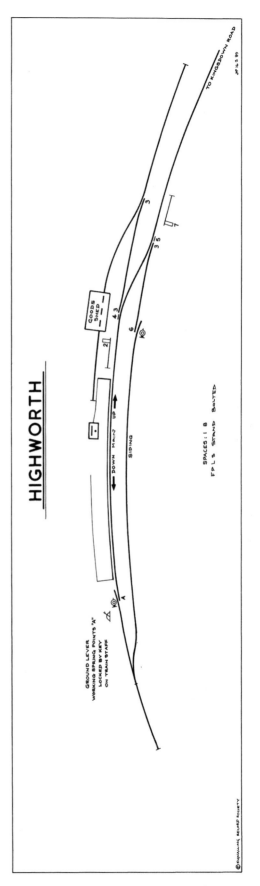

Highworth station, 1910–62.

Highworth Junction

The original signal box installed in 1874 stood at approximately 76 miles 29 chains and was named 'Swindon 'A'. It was a timber building erected by the signalling contractor Saxby & Farmer and contained thirty levers.[1] The purpose of the box was to control access to the Down side broad /standard gauge transfer sidings and the exit from the Up side transfer sidings. These extensive sidings and large goods shed became necessary when the Gloucester and South Wales line route was converted to standard gauge and the mixed gauge came west from Didcot in 1872.

The GWR general manager, Mr Grierson, wrote to the Board of Trade on 3 July 1873 to advise that the new sidings were ready for use 'and we are anxious to commence to use them without delay. As we are so short of accommodation at Swindon we hope that the Board of Trade will sanction their immediate use and we will comply with any requirement which Captain Tyler may make on his inspection.'[2]

The 'A' box had enough spare levers to take on the function of a junction when the Highworth branch opened on 9 May 1883 but was replaced in June 1914 with a handsome GWR brick signal box containing a 58-lever frame under a hip-gabled roof. In February 1933 an 80-lever frame was installed, which suggests that the signal box was extended at one end.[3] Additions to the layout continued especially during the Second World

A pannier tank propels wagons down the Highworth branch, away from the main line: the Down branch starting signal in the middle distance is lowered. Another pannier is shunting in sidings beside the main line on 14 May 1955. R.C. RILEY/TRANSPORT TREASURY

No. 3717 City of Truro was propelled past Highworth Junction signal box on its way to a siding in the goods yard, near the Cricklade Road, where it could be winched onto a lorry to be taken to the GWR Museum in Faringdon Street in April 1965.

For a mile eastward out of Swindon station the running lines were flanked by acres of sidings: wagon works, Cocklebury yard and the gasworks on the Up side, the 'transfer' on the Down with a large goods shed and a warehouse for the W.D. & H.O. Wills tobacco company. No. 3717 is seen here being hauled towards Highworth Junction with the gasworks in the background.

War. On 31 May 1964 the conventional double track junction was re-laid as a 'single lead' junction.[4] The signal box was taken out of use on 3 March 1968.[5]

Swindon Goods Yard

The original box here, installed in 1874 on the Up side at 76 miles 64 chains was called Swindon 'B'. It was a few yards east of the Cricklade Road bridge. The building is thought to have been a Saxby & Farmer timber construction. It held an eighteen-lever frame and controlled points out of the Down side transfer sidings, and to and from the Up and Down mains to the Up sidings.[1] In 1892 the existing standard gauge siding from the locomotive works and engine shed

CENTRE RIGHT: A view of the west end of Swindon goods yard and the signal box in April 1965.

No. 5067 'St Fagan's Castle' on humble duties, drawing up at the signal on the Down goods loop at Swindon goods yard with a freight from Reading.

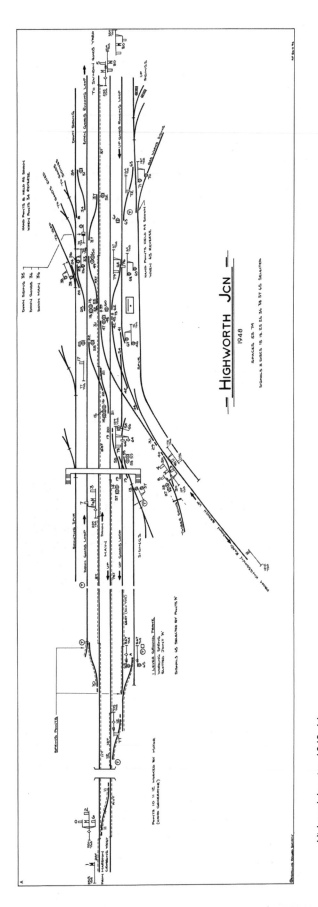

Highworth Junction. 1948–64.

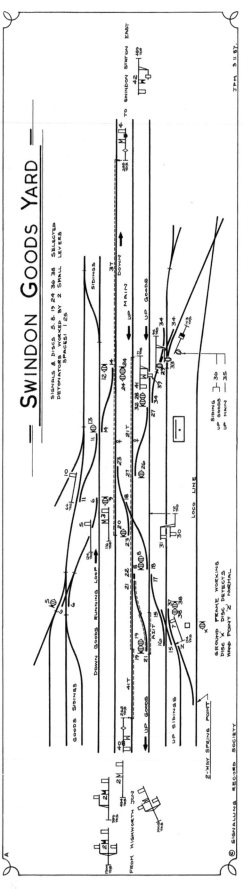

Swindon goods yard, 1930–65.

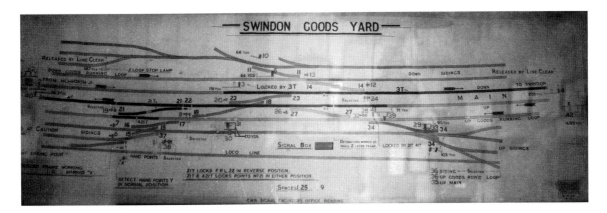

The track diagram, 1963.

No. 92219 heads east through Swindon goods yard with a heavy express freight in 1964. The '92xxx' class were the last steam engines to be designed in Britain and the most powerful class of steam locomotive in Britain at that time. 92219 was built at Swindon. E.J. NUTTY

to its exit at 'B' box had the broad gauge rail added throughout and onto the Up main at 'B' box. This was to allow broad gauge stock to be backed into the siding and taken down to the dump at the west end of the factory.[2] In 1892 a new GWR-design signal box was erected.[3] In January 1909 it was re-named 'Swindon goods yard signal box' and on 26 August 1916 it was replaced with a timber signal box with 42 levers. It was taken out of use on 3 March 1968.[4]

Swindon Station East

The original 1874 signal box controlling the east end of Swindon station was 'C' box. It was a Saxby & Farmer wooden box with outside steps at the station end up to the operating floor. It had fifty-one levers when it opened – including ten spare – and stood on the Up side of the line almost in the mouth of the bay lines.[1] It controlled the east end of the station, and the east-facing bay lines in the Up side and in the Down side platforms 'C' box worked with 'D' to the west and "B" to the east. Each bay had one passenger platform, a 'middle siding' and an engine siding which passed through a 'coaling house' to the buffers.

In 1874 there was no passenger or goods train access at 'C' box from the Down main to the Gloucester branch nor was there access from the Down main for any train to what, in present living memory, was the Down Gloucester branch platform. A track's width to the south of the Down bay was a large goods shed with two sidings passing through it, one on each side of an internal platform. The sidings came from the goods yard and transfer sidings. After passing through the goods shed they merged into a single track and ran across a wagon turntable which allowed trucks to be passed to and from the middle siding of the bay and then alongside the Gloucester branch platform. Mid-way along, forking left, was a siding leading into a carpenters' workshop. At the west end the track went across all running lines to the Gloucester branch or a train could be turned onto the Down Bristol line.[2]

In 1883 the Down bay tracks were lifted and the bay fenced off on both sides. The goods shed to the south was demolished and 'H' box was brought into use with four or five working levers. It stood at about 77 miles 20 chains on the Down side and controlled access from the Down main to what was now the Down Gloucester branch platform. An extra signal was added to 'C' box Down home, this signal was 'slotted' (also controlled by) by 'H' box.[3]

In August 1904 the Down main platform was lengthened which brought about alterations to the tracks, and the points and signals were added. The new work was inspected by Major Pringle on 30 April 1905. His report stated that 'C' box now had 'fifty-one levers, all working'.[4] On 22 January 1909 'C' box was renamed 'Swindon Station East'.[5] Starting in October 1909 the Up platform was extended with the necessary alterations to the tracks. A new all-timber signal box, Swindon

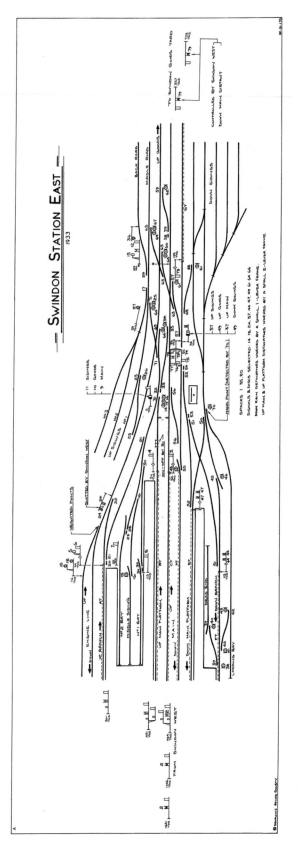

Swindon East 1933–68.

ABOVE: Swindon station looking west from 'C' box, c. 1890. 'H' box can be seen on the left.

RIGHT: Swindon Station East box seen from a departing Up trains, c. 1960.

The station pilot is about to propel a transfer trip down the through line of the station from Swindon East box on 26 April 1959. The right-hand 'calling on' arm is lowered. Arms on the central post route trains to the Down platform; the left-hand arms to the Gloucester Branch platform. The engine has 'Pilot' headcode: one red light, one white at front and rear. *R.C. RILEY/TRANSPORT TREASURY*

Looking east from Swindon East Box. Acres of 'Cocklebury sidings' off to the left, 1962.

The 3.55pm Paddington–Cardiff 'Capitals United Express' passing Swindon East behind a 'Britannia' Pacific, c. 1957. PETER BARLOW

Station East, was brought into use on 13 March 1910 on the Down side at 77 miles 12 chains, replacing Swindon 'C' and Swindon 'H'.[6] It had a frame of sixty-nine working levers plus two spares and nine spaces.[7] The frame was later extended to eighty levers. Early in the Second World War a bomb blast protection wall was built around the lower half of the building. The signal box was closed on 3 March 1968.[8]

Swindon Station West

Swindon 'D' box was opened in 1874, on the Up side at about 77 miles 27 chains. It was a Saxby & Farmer timber production with sixty-six levers.[1] In May 1905 Major Pringle inspected the altered layout after the Down platform was lengthened and reported that the lever frame held sixty-nine levers, five of which were spare.[2] 'D' box worked with 'C',

'E', 'F' and 'H' box. 'D' box controlled a west-facing bay on the Down and Up sides: the latter seems to have been for storing empty carriages. Access to the Gloucester branch at the west end of the station was through facing points at end of the Down main platform line. These points led trains onto the Down bay lines which then merged with the Gloucester Branch platform track and so to the Gloucester branch or to the Down Bristol line. There was no facing connection to the branch from the Down main. On 22 January 1901 the box was renamed Swindon Station West and on 27 October 1912 it was replaced by an all-timber signal box called Swindon Station West on the Down side at 77 miles 33 chains.

It had 163 levers to take over the layouts of the old 'D' box and 'E' box. Eleven levers were added in 1932 – but there was still no facing point from the Down main to the Gloucester Branch: that was not installed until December 1941.[3] A bomb blast protection wall was built around the lower part at the start of the Second World War.

The big Swindon boxes were all busy places to operate but Swindon West box was the most formidable. Three signalmen and a lad telegraphist worked it with an inspector as traffic regulator at busy periods. The signalling regulations were only part of their job. The signalmen had to have the

Swindon West box in 1961. The signalmen retired so as not to obscure the magnificent array of levers. What a wonderful place to work.

entire 24-hour timetable in their heads and then they had to know what each train would do at the station: changing engines, taking on or putting off vehicles. They had to know every detail of the station working and pamphlets laying out what

Steam engines are required for the best atmosphere. Here, the 8am Cheltenham–Paddington passing Swindon West and going through non-stop on the Up main in 1960. This was the only scheduled passenger train off the Gloucester line to do that. DENNIS COTTEREL

each train had to do were regularly produced. The signalmen also had eight shunting engines working in the Works on each side of the line. The shunters would phone – or ring a bell code on a telephone – asking to cross tracks with 'trips' from and to the various workshops. The signalmen had to know the train service, look at the clock, and calculate when that 'trip' could be made.

They had to plan ahead and time a movement in order not to delay the next main line train. So long as it was a steam railway, the traffic could not have been dealt with by a computer. Too much improvisation was required, too much quick thinking and organization: a computer does what it is preplanned to do. With their own brains and with their muscles they operated as a team this vast locking machine with more tracks and train movements within their control than all the tracks and trains on the Swindon Panel control room of 1968 which abolished Swindon West along with the others, on 3 March 1968.

A salute from the happy fireman of a Churchward 'Mogul' as they set off bravely with a clear road out of the area in 1961. The distant signal lowered means that the signals are cleared all the way through Rushey Platt Junction.

Looking due north from Swindon West box to the No. 15 machine shop in April 1965. The nearest signals are the Up platform line starting and Up platform line to Up main starting. Beyond that is a signal for Up engine line/Up engine line to sidings junction signal.

The view north-east over hundreds of acres of wagon works and sidings from Swindon West box in April 1965.

BELOW: Swindon station from West box in 1963.

No. 7016 'Chester Castle' has the signal to turn in from Up main to Up platform at Swindon West on 16 August 1953. The leading coach is of 1906 design. G.W. SHARPE/COLOUR RAIL

A typically grimy '28'-class goods engine reverses along the Up Engine Line going to pick up a train in the goods Yard in 1964. Swindon West box has now lost the junction from Up Gloucester line to the Up main.

Two 'Grange'-class engines and a '97'-class condensing pannier tank – for use in the tunnels of the 'Circle Line', on Acton to Smithfield meat trains – are standing outside the chief mechanical engineer's block in 1964. One 'Grange' is overhauled, but the other is for scrap.

No. 7014 'Caerhays Castle' leaving Swindon station behind and heading west past the 19th-century carriage and wagon works, c. 1953. The railway was everywhere full of fine engineering, interesting and handsome variety.

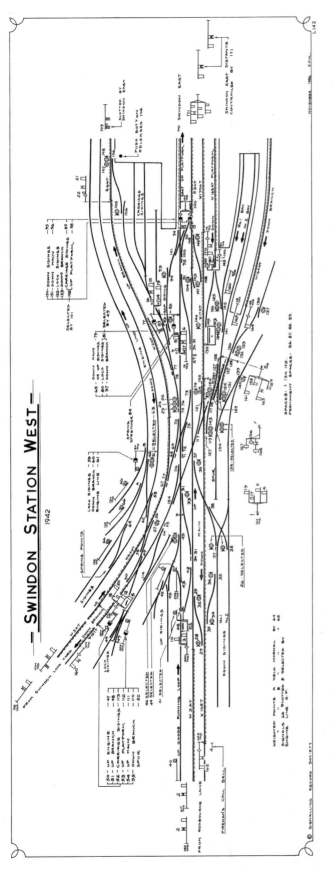

Swindon West 1942–68.

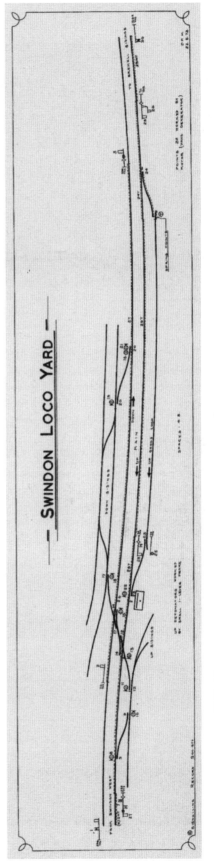

Swindon locomotive yard, 1942–65.

'Acheron' was of the broad gauge 'Hawthorn' class. It started work in February 1866 and was scrapped June 1887. It is seen here outside the Swindon 'E' cabin: a good view of a GWR/Saxby & Farmer signal box with the telegraph boy on the left and signalman on the right, and the 'Lion's Head' emblem on the centre pillar. This was transferred to Swindon West box until 1968.

Swindon 'E'

Swindon 'E', erected in 1874, stood in the 'V' between the Main line and Gloucester branch, on the Down side of the branch. This too was a timber Saxby & Farmer job with forty levers, two being spare. It routed Up branch trains into the Up branch platform or to the Up main Line, not, to the Up main platform.[4] It controlled the Down branch, the engine lines to and from the locomotive depot, the exit of the Up goods loop and sidings to and from the works. It was renamed 'Gloucester Junction' in 1909.

Swindon Locomotive Yard

Before there was a signal box in this area, at 77 miles 60 chains, there were several connections into and across the Gloucester line from the factory on the Down side and from the engine shed vicinity of the 77¾ mile post from early times. These several connections were controlled by levers in a ground frame which was not interlocked with 'E' box but included in its lever frame two levers to control the Up and Down Gloucester line signals worked by 'E' box.[1]

Swindon Locomotive Yard signal box with signalman George Young at the window in 1963.

George Young and his equipment in 1963. The block indicators are GWR 1905 pattern, with their bells alongside. Behind him is the 'hurdy-gurdy' Westinghouse hand generator to make the current to drive the remote point motors on the goods loop points.

A signal box was erected here, on the Up side, in 1876 or 1877. It was a wooden building with plain gables, containing 18 levers.[2] A new frame of twenty-seven levers was installed around 1905. On 27 January 1924 a new signal box, all timber with plain gables, was erected at 77 miles 64 chains with a frame of thirty levers.[3] It stood on the Up side on the embankment, above the engine shed. It survived here until the installation of power signalling on 29 June 1968.[4]

Swindon Running & Maintenance Depot

Sunday afternoon in Swindon shed yard, the air thick with sulphurous yellow smoke as the engines slowly get up steam for work on a Monday morning in 1963.

On the same smoky Sunday, at the shed door end of the line, smokeboxes – and at the far end an interloper.

The locomotive shed consisted of two buildings – the original 'Dean' shed, nearest the Gloucester branch and the 'Churchward shed attached to the east wall of that. In the Churchward shed, 3812 and 73027 are having fitters' attention in 1963. A set of piston valves lies on the floor while the fitter goes off to fetch new rings for it.

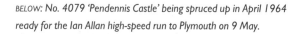

BELOW: No. 4079 'Pendennis Castle' being spruced up in April 1964 ready for the Ian Allan high-speed run to Plymouth on 9 May.

ABOVE: Swindon shed in 1963. Looking in towards the central turntable.

LEFT: Just out of the factory and awaiting work. 7024 will delight the spotters with its appearance on a stopping train between Swindon and Didcot or Swindon and Bristol. The big '72' wasn't given any running-in, he was only going to go slowly on a coal train.

Rodbourne Lane

Rodbourne Lane signal box was one of the 1874 signal box installations. It was then called 'F' box and stood on the Up side of the Bristol line on the western edge of the Rodbourne Lane underbridge, at approximately 77 miles 75 chains.[1] On 5 August 1912 it was replaced by a timber box on the Down side at 78 miles 1 chain. It had a 31-lever frame. The signalman had a splendid view of the 'A' erecting shop and worked, amongst other things, a complex 'ladder' crossover connecting Works sidings on both sides of the line to the main lines, goods loops and engine lines. The box was taken out of use on 1 March 1968.[2]

RIGHT: Opposite 'A' shop in 1962 and a bit to the east stood Rodbourne Lane signal box giving the signalman a wonderful view of the Works and with 'soled and heeled' engines emerging every day and occasionally, the start of a special 'trials' run.

BELOW: The interior of Rodbourne Lane with George Young again, in 1962. His left hand is resting between a GWR 1947 permissive block instrument and the bell by which messages applying to that track are sent. Next along is a GWR/Tyer's permissive block instrument, clearly from a more expansive, Edwardian period. Then there is the block switch for switching this box out of circuit, the GWR 1905 block instruments working with Rushey Platt Junction and Swindon West box and finally another Tyer's for the Up goods loop to Swindon West.

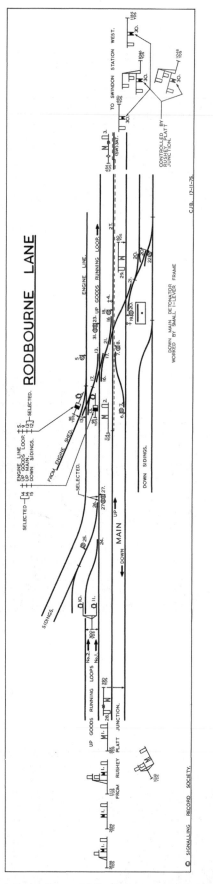

Rodbourne Lane, c. 1941–68.

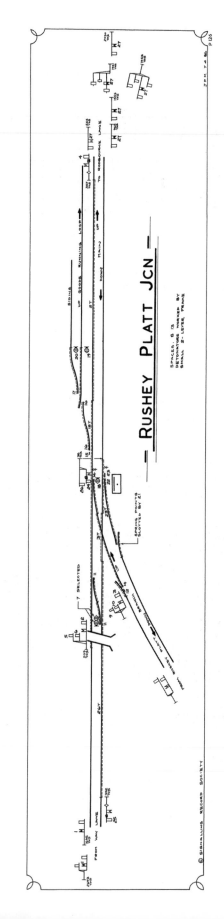

Rushey Platt Junction, c. 1953.

138

Swindon Works

ABOVE: Swindon Works 'A' shop: the place where the locomotives were 'erected' – put together using the boilers and mechanical parts which had been refurbished in the various machine shops, foundries and forges making up the superb Swindon Works.

BELOW: The broad gauge 'North Star' in 1962. This is part replica and part original. It was one of the first engines on the GWR in 1837, and the only good one at the time. It was designed at Robert Stephenson's works in Newcastle. The others were built in Liverpool to Mr Brunel's specifications. Mr Churchward ordered its scrapping in 1906 but the chaps in the Works dismantled it and hid the bits. In 1925 it was re-assembled for the Stockton & Darlington centenary celebrations.

ABOVE: First turned out of 'A' Shop in July 1927, No. 6002 turned out, 'soled and heeled' for the last time early in 1962. The engine was withdrawn for scrapping in September 1962 and torched at Cox & Danks, Oldbury, the following February.

ABOVE RIGHT: Engines stripped to frames, engines re-painted: all stages of overhaul. 3218 was one that was rebuilt and scrapped before going back into service because the line it was destined to work had closed under the Beeching proposals.

RIGHT: No. 4157 2-6-2 tank engine in 'A' shop. The '41xx' were passenger or freight engines. 4157 ended its time, as a Severn Tunnel banker, in June 1965.

No. 6009 'King Charles II' built here in 'A' shop in March 1928, under overhaul in early 1962. In the changeover from steam to diesel, problems with the supply of more diesels and the failures of those that were at work, kept many steam engines running beyond the time planned by Western Region. No. 6009 went in the great slaughter of September 1962 and was torched at Cashmores in December.

Powerful 2-6-2 tank engine 6111 went to Oxford from Works and was among the last of the Western Region steam engines to be withdrawn, in December 1965. 6974 Bryngwyn Hall went to Old Oak Common shed and did wonders of speed on the Paddington–Worcester expresses, substituting for unreliable or absent 'Hymek' diesels. It ended its career at Oxford in May 1965.

ABOVE: No. 92205 erecting in 'A' shop. The magnificent '92' class lasted five to eight years before scrapping.

ABOVE LEFT: No. 6155, 2-6-2 tank was sent from the Works to Worcester. Scrapped October 1965.

The '6959' class of 'Halls', of which 7907 was one, were being overhauled till quite late in the steam era in order to keep express services running on the Worcester–Paddington route. No. 4160 is now preserved on the West Somerset Railway.

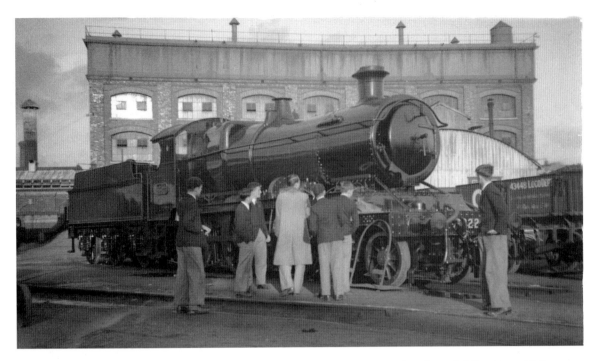

No. 6322 standing by the Works turntable, in front of the Pattern Stores, admired by a group of Marlborough College boys in 1936.
R.H.N. HARDY

Rushey Platt Junction (GWR)

The signal box here, on the Up side at 78 miles 42 chains, was brought into use on 6 February 1882 by the GWR on behalf of, and paid for by, the Swindon, Marlborough & Andover Railway Company (SMAR) which used the Down bay platform at Swindon Junction. The signal box was an all-timber Gloucester Carriage & Wagon

Company production accommodating eighteen levers to control the junction turning south to the Swindon Town station of the SMAR.[1] It was named 'Swindon 'K'' by the GWR until 1900 when it got its final title.

In March 1914 a new GWR pattern signal box was brought into use on the Down side at about the same mileage. It held eleven levers but the floor was long enough to take a 27-lever frame. On

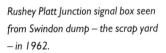

Rushey Platt Junction signal box seen from Swindon dump – the scrap yard – in 1962.

No. 3854, a good, steady old nag, heads for Wootton Bassett past Rushey Platt Junction with an 'F' headcode goods, signalled with 3-2 beats on the bells through the signal boxes. *R.C. RILEY/TRANSPORT TREASURY*

7 June 1921 such a frame was installed to control access to an Up goods loop and Up siding.[2] At the start of the Second World War a brick bomb-blast protection was built around the lower half. English bond brickwork was used in all these blast protection walls because of the great strength of that form of bricklaying.

The box was taken out of use on 4 March 1968 when Swindon Panel took over the signalling of trains.[3]

Rushey Platt Junction (M&SW)

The SMAR ran to and from Swindon Town and Swindon Junction from 6 February 1882 until 28 February 1885. The Swindon & Cheltenham Extension Railway Company built the route north, bridging the GWR, and the two companies merged under the title Midland & South Western Junction Railway (MSWJR) on 23 June 1884. The M&SW joined the GWR route from Banbury to

Rushey Platt Junction looking east from the Midland & South Western Junction Railway bridge. H.F. WHEELER/R.S. CARPENTER COLLECTION

Looking down the 1 in 70 gradient towards the GWR main line at Rushey Platt Junction with the ex-MSWJR heading north on the left on 8 September 1961. Rushey Platt station signal box in the distance from where these points are controlled.
JAMES HAROLD/TRANSPORT TREASURY

Looking north to Rushey Platt Junction signal box on the MSWJR main line to Cirencester and Cheltenham, c. 1925. L&GRP

Cheltenham at Andoversford and joined the Midland Railway at Lansdown Junction. The connection was opened at Cheltenham on 1 August 1891. Thus there was a tremendous fall – or climb – from the crest of the Cotswolds at Foss Cross the bottom of the Severn Valley at Lansdown Junction.

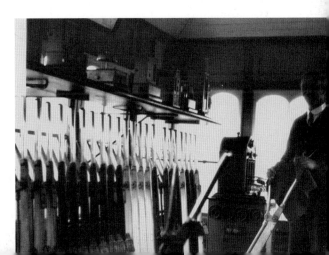

RIGHT: *Interior of Rushey Platt Junction box, c. 1925: Saxby & Farmer frame and GWR signalling instruments. L&GRP*

143

The signal box originally provided by the M&SWR at their Rushey Platt Junction was a wooden Gloucester Carriage & Wagon building. This was replaced in 1917 with an all-brick signal box with distinctly London & South Western Railway features and a Stevens thirty-lever frame; six were spares.[1] The new box had a frame of thirty Saxby & Farmer levers of which twenty-four were working. The layout was remarkable with two double tracks merging into a single line and with some complicated arrangements of trap points to prevent trains from colliding side-on or head-on. During two great wars this thoroughly rural railway was of the utmost importance to the war effort. It served the huge military area of Tidworth and Ludgershall and it carried troops and munitions between the industrial Midlands and north and Southampton. Locally at least it was legendary for the traffic it carried, including hundreds of squaddies on their nights out in Swindon. It had various affection nicknames: the Piss and Vinegar out of respect for the khaki-clad revellers going back to barracks after a night out and the 'Tiddley Dyke'. Its initials earned the soubriquet, the Milk & Soda Water.

Rushey Platt (MSWJR) signal box was taken out of use on 4 June 1965.[2]

Swindon Town station, ex-Midland & South Western Junction Railway. Looking south off the Devizes Road bridge in March 1962.

Swindon Town 'A' and 'B'

These two SMAR signal boxes opened on 26 July 1881. They were all-timber Gloucester Carriage & Wagon Company buildings.[1] The London & South Western Railway (LSWR) was also interested in this optimistic railway route, and traffic became so brisk that in 1904–5 Swindon Town station was enlarged and two new signal boxes were built to an L&SWR design.

Swindon 'A'

The 'A' box, at the north end of the station, was a red-brick L&SWR lookalike, with hipped gables, and the 'B' box was the same design but in timber for lightness because it was perched on the edge of a high embankment at the south end. The 'A' box

Swindon Town 'A', March 1962.

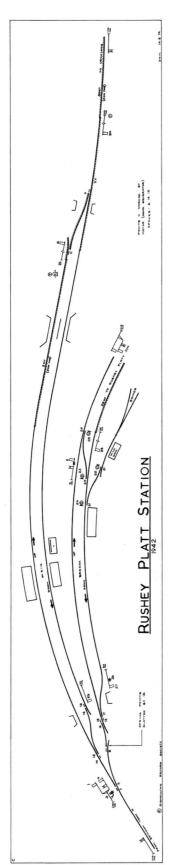

Rushey Platt Station in 1942. M&SW

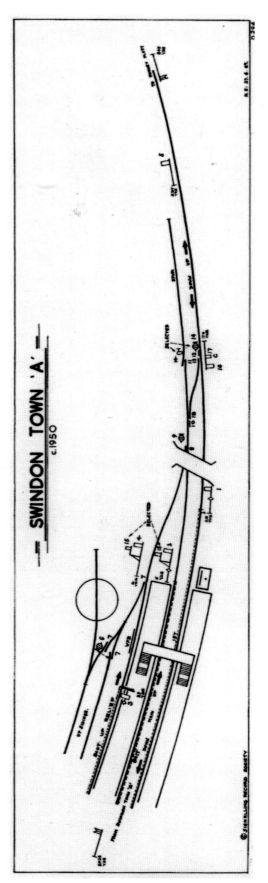

Swindon Town 'A' in 1950.

Swindon Town looking north in March 1962.

LEFT: Swindon Town 'B' box, March 1962.

was equipped with Saxby & Farmer frame of seventeen levers, two spares. At the start of the Second World War the track layout at Swindon Town was enlarged slightly requiring five more levers. There were already the two spares and two more levers were made available by fixing the Up and Down distant signals at 'caution' so one more lever was made to work two ground signals: one or the other moved when the lever was pulled, depending on which set of points had been reversed.

In June 1954 a GWR 27-lever frame was installed, twenty-six working, when an additional facing crossover was added.[2]

Swindon 'B'

'B' box had a 27-lever, one spare, Saxby & Farmer frame installed in 1905 and this was replaced with a 45-lever GWR frame in September 1942. The line closed to passenger traffic on 9 September 1961, but goods traffic kept both boxes open until 9 March 1964.[3]

Swindon Town 'B' GWR wooden Up starting signals and GWR 1942 tubular steel, Down inner home signals, March 1962.

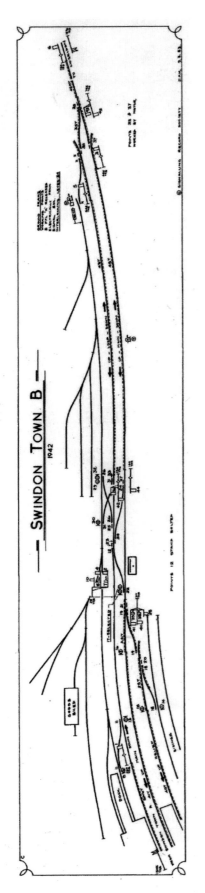

Swindon Town 'B', 1942–61.

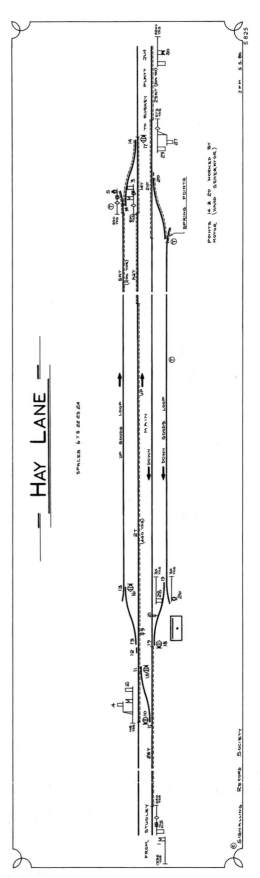

Hay Lane, 1941–68.

Hay Lane

Hay Lane signal box was installed in 1874 on the Down side at 79 miles 62 chains. Most probably to the usual GWR design for small signal boxes of that first period. It held a ten-lever frame to operate three signals on each track, and the points and exit signals for Up and Down refuge siding.[1] The ground signals for entering the sidings would have been turned by the movement of the point blades. The length of the refuge sidings was increased in August 1904 and the signal box was extended in August 1915 to accommodate a fifteen-lever frame.[2] The GWR must have had plans to install a main to main crossover but nothing was done to the layout.

On 1 June 1941 a new Hay Lane signal box was opened on the Down side at 80 miles. This was built, surprisingly for wartime, to the classic hip-gabled, brick design. It held a frame of thirty levers to control the main lines and the entrance and exits to an Up and a Down goods loop.[3] The signal box stood at the western end of the loops which extended eastwards 880yd so the east end points were worked by hand-generated electricity using a 'hurdy-gurdy machine that would have been a heavy churning job. The loops were taken out of use on 27 September 1964 and the signal box was closed on 24 March 1968.[4]

Studley

Studley was a timber-built 'break section' box containing a nine-lever frame to operate six running signals and a crossover road with independent discs. It was brought into use on the Up side at 81 miles 42 chains on 26 April 1904.[1] It almost exactly halved the block section between Hay Lane and Wootton Bassett East. These break section boxes were part of the new Great Western: the construction of new main lines, more goods loops, more powerful engines and higher speeds. Having block posts every 1½ to 2½ miles apart, and high capacity goods loops, more trains could use the tracks without causing delays. Studley was closed on 26 April 1953,[2] when it was replaced by colour-light distant and home signals operated from Hay Lane, on the Down line and Wootton Bassett East on the Up.

Wootton Bassett East and West

On 24 June 1873, Colonel Yolland inspected a new refuge siding at Wootton Bassett. It lay alongside, and was connected to, the Up main to the west of the station. There was already a refuge siding on the south side. Yolland reported that: 'The company is proposing to interlock the whole of the points and

No. 4089 'Donnington Castle' with the Kensington–Whitland milk empties has just passed Hay Lane signal box in May 1957. DON LOVELOCK

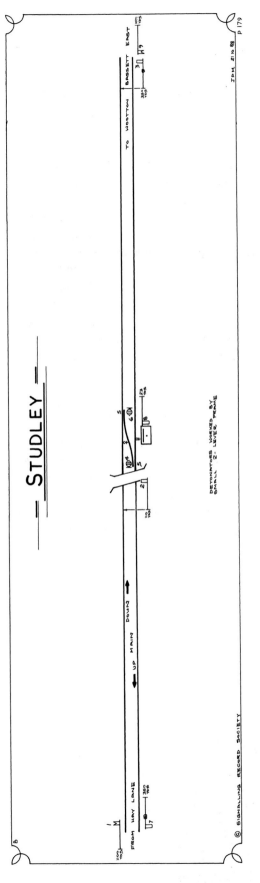

STUDLEY

Studley, 1904–53.

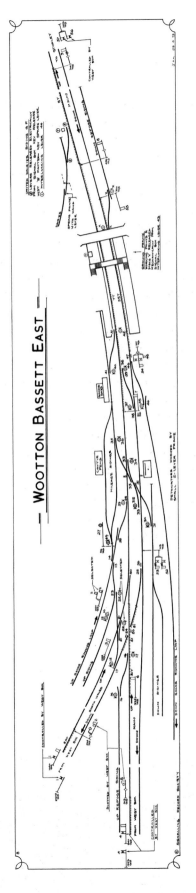

WOOTTON BASSETT EAST

Wootton Bassett East 1907–66/68 (the date of closure of United Dairies is uncertain).

Wootton Bassett new station shortly before the opening of the 'South Wales Direct' line in 1903. There are 'not in use' crosses on the right-hand signal arms.

No. 7021 'Haverfordwest Castle' comes through Wootton Bassett with a train of mostly GWR carriages, apparently coasting for the 50mph restriction over the junction curve: the driver is taking his ease, c. 1955.
DON LOVELOCK

signals at the station.'[1] A signal box was brought in by March 1874.[2] It was the standard design brick building but it was placed gable end-on to the Down main line and stood at the foot of the platform ramp.

Interlocking is a great advance for safety but safety also depends on the driver seeing and acting upon the signals. That was as true at Southall in 1997 as at Wootton Bassett early in the morning of 24 November 1887.

That morning the 12.20am Swindon to Bristol goods, consisting of ten loaded and twentysix empty wagons and a brake van at the rear, hauled by a tank engine was being reversed into the Down refuge siding to clear the line for the 11.20pm Paddington (23 November) express goods. Wootton Bassett Down distant and home signals were at 'danger', beyond them was a starting and an advanced starting signal. In order for the siding points lever to be pulled these signals had to be at 'danger'.

The Swindon goods stopped at the advanced starting and the tail of the train was more than 200yd in advance of the home signal which, by the regulations of that time, permitted signalman William Wyatt to accept the 11.20 Paddington from Hay Lane at full 'Line Clear'. This 200yd in advance of the home signal was – and still is – known as the 'clearing point'.

The 11.20 Paddington was hauled by a tender engine with a steam brake. There were forty-four loaded wagons and the brake van. The Wootton Bassett Down distant signal was showing a red light which on that clear night could be seen for 1,000yd before passing it. The Down home could also be seen for 1,000yd before reaching it except that it was obscured by Templar's bridge between 790 and 600yd from reaching it. As the 12.20 Swindon was starting to reverse, the express goods was heard coming, fast. Shortly after the collision took place, the hand signalman, James Wilkins, who was on duty each night to assist the signalman with these shunting moves, asked driver James Hall 'However came you to run in like this?' Driver Hall replied, 'I mistook the signals.'

Driver Hall stated that he was looking out for the distant but never saw it and only saw the home signal at 'danger' after passing under Templar's bridge. He had 600yd in which to stop and hit the Swindon goods at 20mph. He had to take the responsibility for the crash which luckily did not hurt anyone seriously.[3] Maybe it was after this incident that the GWR extended their 'clearing point' to 440yd. Given the lack of brakes on goods trains it is surprising that a 200yd clearing point was ever considered sufficient. If a 440yd clearing point was the regulation in 1887 Wyatt would have accepted the fast goods 'under the warning' which would have brought the train nearly to a stand at Hay Lane and the driver would have been instructed as to the situation at Wootton Bassett.

When Wootton Bassett became the junction for the shortened route to South Wales and Bristol, two signal boxes were required to work the layout: the East box and the West. West box opened first on 17 November 1901.[4] It stood at 83 miles 22 chains and was built to the new standard design, like the stations on the new lines: red brick with blue bricks up all corners and around locking room windows except along the bottom thereof, where there were cast-iron window sills. The roof had hipped gables and slates. West box had a frame of thirty-seven levers, three spare.

The East box was opened on 13 July 1902.[5] It stood at 83 miles and 3 chains from Paddington and thus was only 418yd from West box. It was a handsome timber building – with the same outline as the new brick boxes – holding fifty-seven levers, three of them spare, under a hip gable roof. The East box worked the junction and the sidings nearest the station, the West box, the western extremities of the layout. The new railway was opened throughout on 1 May 1903.[6]

A new Up goods loop for South Wales trains and a new Down goods loop for Bristol line trains were inspected by Colonel Yorke for the Board of Trade on 6 June 1906.[7] Various other sidings, looped sidings and crossovers were added until there was an extensive layout.

Wootton Bassett signalmen had a splendid view of the countryside and of the fastest trains on the Great Western and Western Region. There was no speed limit over the junction for Down trains heading towards Chippenham. Every day the magnificent trains came flying through the station on their 120 minutes schedule for the 118¼ miles

No. 5061 'Earl of Birkenhead' comes round the curve, off the South Wales line, at around 55–60mph and starts to accelerate towards Wootton Bassett station on 25 March 1961. The speed restriction for Up train was less than in the Down direction. The uppermost 'danger' signal is Wootton Bassett East's Down inner home, to the left a signal directing into the Down Bristol line goods loop. The distant signals are Wootton Bassett West's for the Bristol line and the South Wales line. HUGH BALLANTYNE

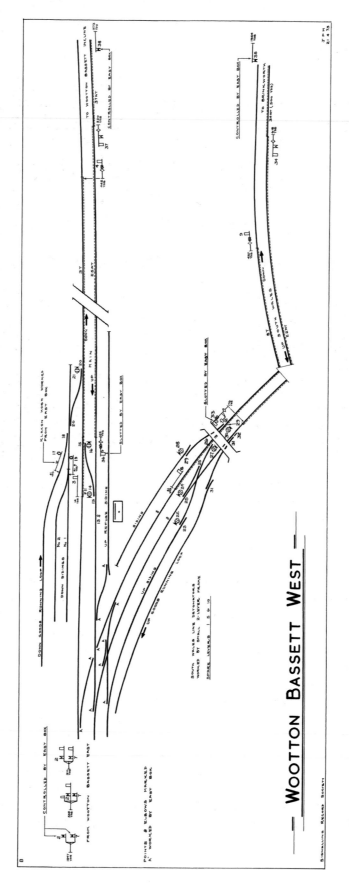

Wootton Bassett West, 1907–64.

No. 4996 'Eden Hall' pilots No. 5092 'Tresco Abbey' with a Down Bristol express, passing Wootton Bassett East's Down starting signal with Wootton Bassett West's inner distant below on 18 September 1955. R.C. RILEY/TRANSPORT TREASURY

Wootton Bassett West box, c. 1947. A grand array of GWR mahogany-cased and brass-cased instruments; gleaming steel lever handles. The signal boxes were glorious places of work in steam days. RAY THOMAS

Track diagram in Wootton Bassett West box, c. 1947. Two GWR brass-cased 'Track clear/occupied' electric indicators on the right. RAY THOMAS

Paddington–Bristol – with a stop at Bath. Express trains for South Wales had to reduce to 40mph but Up South Wales expresses had only to reduce to 60mph.[8]

At 4.7am on 27 June 1946 the 11.50pm Paddington to Carmarthen express freight was derailed on the Wootton Bassett junction at 40mph. The engine overturned and the leading twenty-six wagons piled up onto it and beyond. The general manager's report[9] on this states that 'the guard sustained severe shock and slight injuries to the head and left knee'. The *Bristol Evening News* of 27th stated: 'driver and fireman unhurt'.

The derailment was caused by the cover of the facing point bolt coming off. With the cover removed the normally horizontal bolt was tilted upwards by the weight of the drive rod so that the bolt did not engage in its port. And this had to happen when the blade of the facing point had not fully closed against the rail in obedience to the lever.

There was another crash at Wootton Bassett on 5 September 1961. A Down goods train passed Wootton Basett East box without a brake van. The signalman realized instantly that the train had become divided and the rear part was following, on a gentle downgrade, so he turned the facing points for the Down goods loop to prevent the wagons running away down Dauntsey bank. The wagons crashed through the buffers beyond and spread wagons across the Up and Down main lines.

A Down goods diverted into the Down loop at Wootton Bassett East failed to stop at the exit signal, crashed through the buffers beyond and flung loaded wagons left and right, on 5 September 1961. Wootton Bassett West box is in distance. *DON LOVELOCK*

The facing point bolt: engaged/disengaged.

At the end of eight hours on the track on a hot summer's day, the up-way men gratefully trudge off home as a 'Castle' goes scampering past with a train of mostly GWR coaches, c. 1955. DON LOVELOCK

Notes

Chapter 1

1. Estimating from Ordnance Survey sheet 157.
2. Rail 1149/4, pp.111–116.
3. Rail 1149/44.

Chapter 2

1. Rail 250/117.
2. Rail 1149/5, p.110.
3. *ibid.*, p.120.
4. *ibid.*, p.134.
5. *ibid.*, p.337.
6. Rail 1149/6, pp.42 and 44.
7. *ibid.*, p.59.
8. *Locomotives of the Great Western Railway. Part 2. Broad Gauge* (RCTS).
9. Rail 250/94, p.7.
10. Rail 250/2, p.173.
11. Rail 274/161; 1in to 132ft.
12. Rail 250/3, p.43.
13. *ibid.*, p.61.
14. Rail 250/688, p.37.
15. Rail 250/117.
16. Rail 250/122.
17. Rail 266/46, p.17.

Chapter 3

1. Rail 1008/34, p.39.
2. Rail 250/2, p.142.
3. Rail 250/117.
4. Rail 250/117.
5. Daniel Gooch's evidence to the Gauge Commissioners 1846 in McDermott, E.T., *History of the Great Western Railway*, vol.1, p.434.
6. McDermott, E.T., *History of the Great Western Railway*, Vol.1, p.435.
7. Vaughan, Adrian, *Grub, Water & Relief*, p.71.
8. *ibid.*
9. MT 29/1.
10. Rail 250/126, p.96.
11. Rail 250/116.
12. Rail 250/3.
13. Rail 250/688, p.39.

Chapter 4

1. Gibbons, Agnes, *Wantage Past and Present*, p.93 (1901).
2. Rail 250/123.
3. Rail 250/20, pp.37–38.
4. Rail 250/20, p.93.
5. Rail 250/688, p.37.
6. Rail 250/192, pp.209–210.
7. *Berkshire Chronicle*, 16 December 1965.
8. Rail 937/85 and 115.
9. Rail 267/176.
10. Bagwell, Prof. Philip, *The Railwaymen*, p.544 (George Allen & Unwin).
11. Rail 266/46, p.17.

Chapter 5

1. The original letters relating to this are in the author's collection.
2. Rail 266/46, p.16.
3. Jim Brown's recollections.

Chapter 6

1. Vaughan, Adrian, *A History of Uffington Station and the Faringdon Branch* (Amberley Press).
2. *ibid.*, p.82.
3. Rail 253/453.
4. Rail 266/46, p.68.
5. Rail 253/736.
6. Rail 266/46, p.68.

Chapter 7

1. Rail 250/117.
2. *Berkshire Chronicle*, 19 August 1848 and Rail 250/126, p.36.
3. Rail 1149/2, p.227.
4. Rail 266/46, p.68.

Chapter 8

1. Rail 266/46, p.18.
2. Rail 937/165.
3. Rail 266/46, p.18.
4. *GWR Book of Dates of Acts, Openings and Amalgamations*, compiled by P.R. Gale, Chief Goods Manager's Office, Paddington, 1926. Mr. Gale received £50 for this remarkable compilation covering the entire GWR. A copy is in the author's possession.
5. GWR Appendix to No.4 Section Working Time Table.
6. Signalling Record Society, 'Signal Box Register', p.168, and Cooke, R.A., *Track Layout Diagrams of the Great Western Railway and BR Western Region*, Section 20.
7. *ibid.*
8. *ibid.*
9. Rail 266/46, p.70.

Chapter 9

1. Rail 250/2, p.142. The Cheltenham & Great Western Union Railway (C&GWU) incorporated on 21 June 1836. In April 1840 the Great Western bought a seven-year lease of its route, then nearing completion, from its junction at Swindon to Cirencester.
2. Rail 250/2, p.143.
3. Rail 250/2, p.147.
4. McDermott, vol.1, p.62.
5. Rail 250/2, p.145.
6. Rail 252/194.
7. Rail 1149/6, pp.164–165.
8. Rail 252/194.
9. Rail 250/2, p.152.
10. Cattell, John and Falconer, Keith, *Swindon: The Legacy of a Railway Town*, p.38.
11. *ibid.* p.37.
12. Rail 250/2, pp.158–161.
13. McDermott, E.T., *History of the Great Western Railway*, vol.1, p.72.
14. Rail 250/2, pp.158–161.
15. The full story of this saga can be found in Cattell and Falconer, p.42.
16. Rail 252/174.
17. McDermott, E.T., *History of the Great Western Railway*, vol.1, p.75.
18. Rail 266/46, p.18.
19. Ackworth, W.M., *The Railways of England*.

Chapter 10

1. Rolt, L.T.C., *Isambard Kingdom Brunel*, p.135.
2. Rail 250/117, 27 October 1941.
3. Rail 250/117, 10 March 1942.
4. Rail 250/123, 1 January 1946.
5. Rail 250/3, 11 August 1948.
6. Railway Archives online. Accidents, 29 Oct 1962.
7. *Devizes & Wiltshire Gazette,* 28 March 1967.
8. Rail 250/688.
9. *Encyclopedia of the Great Western Railway* (PSL, 1993), p.221.
10. Rail 266/46.

Chapter 11

Introduction
1. MFQ 1/285.
2. *ibid.*
3. Rail 274/161.

Steventon
1. MT 6/341/5 and SRS Register.
2. MT 6/341/5.
3. Rail 274/161.
4. MT 6/564/3.
5. MT 6/1657/3.
6. SRS Register, p.157.
7. BR(WR) No.4 Section Appendix 1948.

Lockinge
1. SRS Register.
2. Rail 282/104.
3. Rail 250/468.
4. BR(WR) internal report in author's collection.
5. SRS Register.

Wantage Road
1. R.A. Cooke. Section 23, p.2.
2. The Railway Archive online. Board of Trade Report dated 9 January 1915.
3. SRS Register.
4. *ibid.*

Circourt Crossing
1. SRS Register.
2. MT 6/1657/3.
3. *ibid.*
4. Rail 282/106.

Challow
1. Rail 282/106.
2. *ibid.*
3. *ibid.*

Uffington
1. SRS Register.
2. Vaughan, Adrian, *A History of Uffington Station and the Faringdon Branch* (Amberley Press).
3. SRS Register.
4. AN 125/1.
5. Rail 282/107.

Knighton Crossing
1. Rail 250/117.
2. *ibid.*

3. Rail 250/688, pp.2–3.
4. The Signalling Study Group, *The Signal Box: A Pictorial History and Guide to Designs*, p.161.
5. R.A. Cooke. Section 23, p.1.
6. Rail 274/162. GWR 2-chain survey 1936. This reference is incorrectly allocated, at the National Archives, to a different survey.

Ashbury Crossing
1. R.A. Cooke. Section 23. p.1.
2. *ibid.*
3. Rail 282/106 and R.A. Cooke. Section 23. p.1.
4. SRS Register.

Shrivenham
1. SRS Register.
2. R.A. Cooke. Section 23. p.1.
3. *ibid.*
4. MT 61347/10 and MT 6/1385/2.
5. R.A. Cooke. Section 23. p.1.
6. Rail 1053/122 Ministry of Transport Report into the 1936 crash.
7. *ibid.*
8. Rail 250/468.
9. SRS Register.

The Marston Boxes
1. MT 6/329/8.
2. Rail 253/307.
3. R.A. Cooke. Section 23. p.1.
4. *ibid.*
5. SRS Register.

The Highworth Branch
1. R.A. Cooke. Section 20. p.29.
2. *ibid.*
3. The extreme complexity of this area of the Highworth branch can best be appreciated by reading *The Highworth Branch* by T.M. Smith & G.S. Heathcliffe, published by Wild Swan, and looking at 'Track Layout Diagrams of the Great Western Railway and BR Western Region. Section 20: Swindon and South Gloucestershire' by R.A. Cooke.

Highworth Junction

1. SRS Register.
2. MT 6/105/4. This reference in the National Archives catalogue is allocated to Wootton Bassett station 1873.
3. SRS Register.
4. R.A. Cooke. Section 20. p.24.
5. SRS Register.

Swindon Goods Yard

1. SRS Register and MT 6/121/18.
2. MT 6/578/14.
3. R.A. Cooke. Section 20. p.22.
4. SRS Register.

Swindon Station East

1. MT 6/1030/2.
2. Rail 274/161.
3. MT 6/348/9.
4. MT 6/1347/6.
5. R.A. Cooke. Section 20. p.19.
6. SRS Register.
7. MT 6/1961/3.
8. SRS Register.

Swindon Station West

1. SRS Register.
2. MT 6/1347/6.
3. R.A. Cooke. Section 20. p.19.
4. MT 6/348/9.

Swindon Locomotive Yard

1. MT 6/141/15.
2. SRS Register.
3. *ibid.*
4. *ibid.*

Rodbourne Lane

1. Rail 274/161.
2. SRS Register.

Rushey Platt Junction (GWR)

1. Bartholemew, David, *The Midland & South Western Junction Railway*, p.42.
2. SRS Register.
3. *ibid.*

Rushey Platt Junction (M&SW)

1. Bartholemew, David, *The Midland & South Western Junction Railway*, p.84.
2. SRS Register.

Swindon Town 'A' and 'B'

1. Bartholemew, David, *The Midland & South Western Junction Railway*, p.89.
2. SRS Register.
3. *ibid.*

Hay Lane

1. SRS Register.
2. R.A. Cooke. Section 20. p.9.
3. SRS Register.
4. R.A. Cooke. Section 20. p.19.

Studley

1. R.A. Cooke. Section 20. p.19 and SRS Register.
2. *ibid.*

Wootton Bassett East and West

1. MT 6/105/4.
2. MFQ/1/285. GWR Signalling Regulations March 1874.
3. Rail 1053/76.
4. R.A. Cooke. Section 20. p.8.
5. *ibid.*
6. McDermott, E.T., *History of the GWR*, vol.2, p.321.
7. MT 6/1481/12.
8. GWR Working Time Table 1936.
9. Rail 250/468.

Index

Acorn bridge, Brunel and   59–60

Brown, Jim, recollections of Challow
  station   45–47
Brunel, Isambard, Kingdom, designed the Vale
  route   9
  reasons for broad gauge   9
  signalling, Brunellian   31–32
  underestimates costs of construction   70
  vendetta against Freeman   17
  wants a deviation   12, 57

Carriages, early types described   30–31
  lack of brakes   31
Challow station, drinking water tank   41–42
  7.20 Cheltenham express   48
  a local institution   42–44
  closure of   48
  'Duchess', shunting horse   43
  during WW2   45
  Harry Strong at Challow   43
  Jimmy Titchener, lampman   45
  rebuilding of   43
  Station Master Gardiner, chapel coach   42–43
  Station Master Francis   47
  statistics of   47
Cheltenham & Great Western Union Railway,
  Swindon   67–68
Contractors for construction   13
  William Ranger   59–60

Electric telegraph   31–32

Faringdon branch, opened   49
  closure to goods traffic   55
  closure to passengers   55
  described   49–50
  engine shed   51
  military manouvres over   51–52
  report on profitability   53–54
  train service, traffic, on   52–55
  Train Staff safety system   50–51
Faringdon Road station and site described   26–27
  Constable Clewitt, charged   32

fatal crashes at   28–29, 32–33
  goods shed blown down   29
  importance of   28
  re-named 'Challow'   41
  staff wages   28
Faringdon station, statistics   54

Gandell, J.H., designs Steventon permanent
  buildings   16
  contractor for Hay Lane station   68
  owner of Hay Lane station buildings   69
Great Western Railway, first use of title   9
  'gentleman's railway'   30
  high speed trains   31
  no money to build Swindon station, Works and
  housing   70
  vital importance of   40

Hay Lane 'principal passenger station' for
  Swindon   67–68
  'engine station' to be established   67
  inspecting Officer's report on   68
  John Streat, sub-contractor for   68
  route opened to   68–69
Highworth branch, route described   63–64
  in Great War   65
  in WW2   66
  public passenger service withdrawn   66
  statistics   66
  train service   65

Locomotives: Charon, performance on opening
  train   21
  cabless   31

Mixed gauge, installed   72

Shrivenham station, described   56–57
  closed   60
  Constable Quarrington, exonerared   57
  fatal collision, 1848   57–59
  fatal derail, 1936   114
  staff pay 1863   60
  statistics   60

Signal boxes erected, 'open block' 79–80
  'absolute block' 80
  original sequence of 80
Signal boxes, total
  Ashbury Crossing 111–113
  Challow 92–96
  Circourt Crossing 91
  Hay Lane 147–148
  Highworth branch boxes 120–121
  Highworth Junction 122–124
  Knighton Crossing 106, 108–110
  Lockinge; Lockinge East, Lockinge West 84–86
  Marston Crossing East 117–120
  Rodbourne Lane, including 'F' box 137–138
  Rushey Platt Junction, GWR 141–142
  Rushey Platt Junction, M&SWJR 142–143
  Shrivenham 113–117
  Steventon 81–84
  Studley 148–149
  Swindon 'E' 134
  Swindon Goods Yard 123–124
  Swindon Locomotive Yard 134–135
  Swindon Station East 125–128
      including 'C' and 'H' boxes
  Swindon Station West 128–130
      including 'D', 'E', "F" and 'H' boxes
  Swindon Town 'A' 144–146
  Swindon Town 'B' 146–147
  Uffington 98–106
  Wantage Road 87–91
  Wootton Bassett East 148–151
  Wootton Bassett West 151–154
Slip coach, operation, diagrams 104–105
Steventon station, temporary building 14
  as mail train stopping place 22
  Boardroom at, briefly 22
  Directors attend opening of line to 19
  Harry Strong cycles to Steventon 23
  Inspector Wells 23–24
  permanent buildings at 15–16
  staff at, 1863 23
  statistics, 1903–38 24

Stratton Park Halt 61–62
Strikes, lack of 40
Swindon station, locomotive works at 67
  Brunel makes passenger station at
    Swindon 67–68
  first passenger train non-stop through 74
  passenger station at 67
  refreshment rooms, history 70–74
  station described 69–70
  upper storey designed by Francis Thompson 69
Swindon Running & Maintenance shed 135–136
Swindon Locomotive Works 139–140

Rigby, S & J, contractors for building Vale
  stations 70

Uffington station, agreement to build,
  abandoned 27
  closed 55
  income, 1959 55
  station opened 49

Vale route, described 10–13
  antiquated equipment in 1872 79
  refuge sidings installed 80
  signal boxes erected 80

Wantage town, disreputable repute 34
  goods station established 35
  Mr Ormond, petition for station 34–35
Wantage Road, passenger station opened 36
  Board of Trade investigates facilities 39
  district bus service opened 39
  Royal train at 37
  'Slip' coaches at 38
  statistics of 40
  William Ireson, killed 36–37
Wantage Tramway 37–38
Wootton Bassett station, incidents 75–78
  closed 78
  staff pay 1863 78
  statistics 78